Whitman An Official Whit

Adventure Across the National Parks

Collecting 2010-2021 National Park Quarters and Other Coins

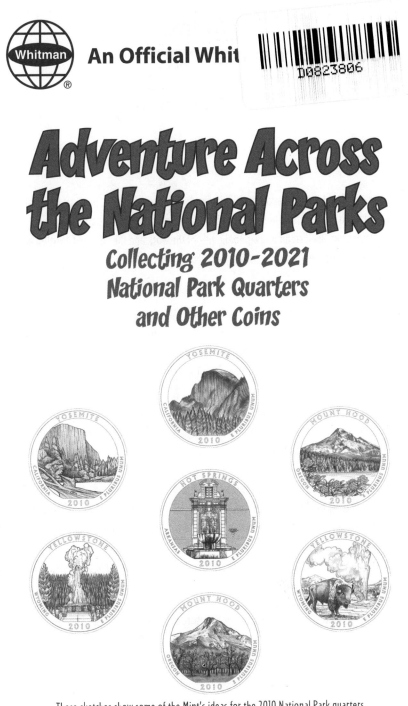

These sketches show some of the Mint's ideas for the 2010 National Park quarters.

Whitman Publishing, LLC
Atlanta, Georgia

www.whitman**books**.com

© 2010 Whitman Publishing, LLC

3101 Clairmont Road · Suite G · Atlanta GA 30329

Correspondence concerning this book may be directed to the publisher, at the address above.

ISBN: 0794828884

Printed in China

Disclaimer: Expert opinion should be sought in any significant numismatic purchase. This book is presented as a guide only. No warranty or representation of any kind is made concerning the completeness or accuracy of the information presented.

If you enjoy *Adventure Across the National Parks*, you will also enjoy *America's Beautiful National Parks: A Handbook for Collecting the New National Park Quarters* (McKeon); *The Inside Story of the State Quarters* (Bowers); and *Adventure Across the States: Collecting State Quarters and Other Coins.*

For a complete catalog of numismatic reference books, supplies, and storage products, visit Whitman Publishing online at www.whitmanbooks.com.

This product is not affiliated with, endorsed by, or sponsored by the National Park Service.

CONTENTS

LIST OF HONORED SITES, BY STATE

Alabama (2021) — Tuskegee Airmen National Historic Site

Alaska (2012) — Denali National Park and Preserve

American Samoa (2020) — National Park of American Samoa

Arizona (2010) — Grand Canyon National Park

Arkansas (2010) — Hot Springs National Park

California (2010) — Yosemite National Park

Colorado (2014) — Great Sand Dunes National Park

Connecticut (2020) — Weir Farm National Historic Site

Delaware (2015) — Bombay Hook National Wildlife Refuge

District of Columbia (2017) — Frederick Douglass National Historic Site

Florida (2014) — Everglades National Park

Georgia (2018) — Cumberland Island National Seashore

Guam (2019) — War in the Pacific National Historical Park

Hawaii (2012) — Hawai'i Volcanoes National Park

Idaho (2019) — Frank Church River of No Return Wilderness

Illinois (2016) — Shawnee National Forest

Indiana (2017) — George Rogers Clark National Historical Park

Iowa (2017) — Effigy Mounds National Monument

Kansas (2020) — Tallgrass Prairie National Preserve

Kentucky (2016) — Cumberland Gap National Historical Park

Louisiana (2015) — Kisatchie National Forest

Maine (2012) — Acadia National Park

Maryland (2013) — Fort McHenry National Monument and Historic Shrine

Massachusetts (2019) — Lowell National Historical Park

Michigan (2018) — Pictured Rocks National Lakeshore

Minnesota (2018) — Voyageurs National Park

Mississippi (2011) — Vicksburg National Military Park

Missouri (2017) — Ozark National Scenic Riverways

Montana (2011) — Glacier National Park

Nebraska (2015) — Homestead National Monument of America

Nevada (2013) — Great Basin National Park

New Hampshire (2013) — White Mountain National Forest

New Jersey (2017) — Ellis Island National Monument (Statue of Liberty)

New Mexico (2012) — Chaco Culture National Historical Park

New York (2015) — Saratoga National Historical Park

North Carolina (2015) — Blue Ridge Parkway

North Dakota (2016) — Theodore Roosevelt National Park

Northern Mariana Islands (2019) — American Memorial Park

Ohio (2013) — Perry's Victory and International Peace Memorial

Oklahoma (2011) — Chickasaw National Recreation Area

Oregon (2010) — Mt. Hood National Forest

Pennsylvania (2011) — Gettysburg National Military Park

Puerto Rico (2012) — El Yunque National Forest

Rhode Island (2018) — Block Island National Wildlife Refuge

South Carolina (2016) — Fort Moultrie (Fort Sumter National Monument)

South Dakota (2013) — Mount Rushmore National Memorial

Tennessee (2014) — Great Smoky Mountains National Park

Texas (2019) — San Antonio Missions National Historical Park

U.S. Virgin Islands (2020) — Salt River Bay National Historical Park and Ecological Preserve

Utah (2014) — Arches National Park

Vermont (2020) — Marsh-Billings-Rockefeller National Historical Park

Virginia (2014) — Shenandoah National Park

Washington (2011) — Olympic National Park

West Virginia (2016) — Harpers Ferry National Historical Park

Wisconsin (2018) — Apostle Islands National Lakeshore

Wyoming (2010) — Yellowstone National Park

FOREWORD

When I was young, I desperately wanted to see the giant sequoias in Yosemite National Park. The thought of a tree that could dwarf the big oaks and maples that grew in my neighborhood was fascinating to me. When I actually saw the giant redwoods, they did not disappoint: they are the largest living things on the planet, and they can be two or three thousand years old.

When you see a tree that large, it's difficult not to think about the enormous number of houses that could be made out of its lumber–not to mention toothpicks. But then, of course, the tree would be gone. Who would get excited about seeing the place where the giant redwoods *used* to be, or a picture of the millions of boxes of toothpicks they were turned into?

Making sure that this kind of thing doesn't happen is the essence of what has been called "America's best idea." As a nation, we have decided that certain places are worth more than any one person or company, or even any single generation, could pay to privately own them. They are open for everyone's enjoyment and preserved for future generations.

The U.S. Mint's America the Beautiful Quarters™ Program is a celebration of these national treasures. At the same time, it is a reminder that there is a lot more out there than the better-known places in the western United States. Yes, the titans of the National Park System are represented: Yellowstone, Yosemite, and the Grand Canyon. But this is just the beginning, the trailhead. Every state and territory in the United States is represented, and their sites come from categories you may not have been aware of, including national forests, lakeshores, seashores, historic monuments, and military parks.

As you collect the quarters, be sure to read up on the places they depict–I'm sure they'll surprise you. There are lush rainforests and remote glaciers, glittering ice caves and rolling grasslands, sprawling forests and scenic parkways. There are a few places you are really going to want to drive to and others that you can only see by boat or, better, kayak.

Their stories are the history of the land, from the liquid rock that will pour out of Mount Kilauea tomorrow to the remains of lakes that vanished millennia ago. Once you have collected all 56 quarters, you will have a huge swath of American history under your arm to carry around with you, with its unique combination of bravery, good fortune, tragedy, self-sacrifice, and, above all, the never-ending pursuit of freedom that has made our country great.

You've got a beautiful nation to explore. I hope you enjoy collecting the quarters and getting to know the stories behind them.

Aaron J. McKeon
Syracuse, New York

Aaron J. McKeon is the author of America's Beautiful National Parks: A Handbook for Collecting the New National Park Quarters. *A member of the American Institute of Certified Planners, McKeon focuses his work on innovative ways to strike a balance between the demands of the manmade world and the preservation of natural resources.*

INTRODUCTION

I t's time for an encore! Back in 1999 we were all thrilled when the Treasury department and the U.S. Mint launched the 50 State Quarters™ Program. At the rate of five per year these coins began appearing in pocket change, starting with Delaware. Finally, in 2008, all 50 states had been covered, and it was time for the District of Columbia and the U.S. territories. Today, a collection of these interesting quarters represents dozens of different designs and concepts, each "home grown," so to speak, as they were created by artists within the individual states and other areas.

Now come our quarters focusing on national parks and historical sites. I can hardly wait to see the panorama of motifs that is sure to develop. In looking over the list I see some are quite recognizable. Mount Rushmore is to be honored, perhaps evincing déjà vu, as the same icon appeared on South Dakota's quarter. Yosemite National Park similarly evokes the California quarter (which featured naturalist John Muir as well as Yosemite). After that, it is a free-for-all.

Each of the 56 coins in the series is bound to be exciting. Every one of us will learn something new. Maryland has chosen to commemorate the Fort McHenry National Monument and Historic Shrine, famous for its "Star Spangled Banner"–but what does the actual fort look like? Perhaps we'll see it on the coins. For Everglades National Park, the choice for Florida, will it be an alligator, a tropical bird, or some other wild animal? A number of national forests are to be honored, including Shawnee in Illinois, Kisatchie (I had not heard of this one before!) in Louisiana, and White Mountains in New Hampshire. Will we see stately trees, native birds, rare plants? As the program unfolds we'll all be watching, collecting the coins one by one, and learning their stories. The series extends to 2021, by which time, I am sure, Congress and the Treasury department will have come up with new coinage ideas. Perhaps famous people in American history? Or? What might *you* like to see on our coins? In the meantime, enjoy collecting the 56 National Park quarters and learning more about them in this fun book, *Adventure Across the National Parks*.

Q. David Bowers
Wolfeboro, New Hampshire

Q. David Bowers is the numismatic director of Whitman Publishing, and chairman of Stack's Rare Coins of New York. He has been involved in the hobby for more than 50 years, as an award-winning author, researcher, columnist, auctioneer, and professional coin and currency dealer. He has served in many offices including as president of both the American Numismatic Association (www.money.org) and the Professional Numismatists Guild (www.pngdealers.com).

THE HISTORY OF COINS

When you go shopping at the store, how do you pay for the things you want? You probably use dollar bills. A grownup with a bank account might write a check, or pay with a plastic debit card. In this book, we look at another kind of money, one that people like to *collect* as well as *spend:* coins!

People have been spending coins for almost 3,000 years. Before coins, other valuable items that people used for money included:

    cattle
    bars of salt
    elephant tails
    rare feathers
    wampum

People would also *barter,* or trade, their goods and services. A farmer who grew vegetables, but had no milk, might barter some of his corn for a neighbor's goat. But bartering is not perfect system. I might want some corn, but if the farmer only wants milk, and I don't have a goat, how can I trade with him? Or, what if I have a goat, but the farmer lives a hundred miles away, and I can't get the goat to walk that far?

Around 2,000 B.C., people started using small pieces of bronze for trading, based on weight. Everyone knew that bronze was a valuable metal, so these pieces would be accepted from town to town. They were often made into the shape of cattle, since cows and bulls were recognized as being valuable, and were often bartered for goods and services. Some pieces were small enough to carry around, but a more valuable piece of bronze might be too big to carry easily.

Finally the first real coins were made, in Lydia. This powerful ancient kingdom no longer exists, but it was located in what is now part of the Republic of Turkey. King Ardys built a mint where precious metal was used to make coin-like objects. The king's workers would gather a metal called *electrum,* actually a natural combination of gold and silver, found in the mountains and streams near the mint. They would use fire to make the metal softer, drop the soft metal onto a plate, place a punch over it, and then hit the punch with a

> Money is a "medium of exchange." What does that mean? Basically, money is anything that can be traded for goods (products, like a video game, or a bicycle) or for services (like raking leaves, or taking the trash out).

> Wampum is an Algonquin word that means "white shell beads." Native Americans used seashells to make little beads, and strung them together as necklaces, belts, or long strands. These beads were valuable because they were rare and beautiful.

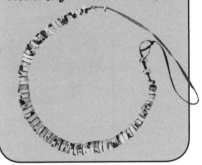

hammer–hard! The punch had a design on it, which would be struck into the metal. The resulting electrum pieces were not like the coins we use today (their sizes and weights were random, and so was the purity of the gold and silver, and they only had a design on one side), but they were close.

When Ardys's son Alyattes became king, he made rules so that Lydia's coins would all have the same weight (168 grains, about the same as two quarter dollars), and also designs on both sides. The 168-grain coins were called *staters*. Later, Alyattes also had his mints make smaller coins.

> **A mint is a building where coins are made.**

When Alyattes's son Croesus became king of Lydia, he made what many people consider the first true official coins. Croesus said "No more electrum," and only allowed gold and silver for his coins. They also had an official design–a lion's head and a bull, symbolizing the strength of his empire. This official design told everyone that the coins were pure gold or pure silver, and that they were authorized by the king.

Since then, coins have been struck by hundreds of kingdoms and other communities, in many metals, shapes, and sizes. In North America, people have used coins since colonial times, and the United States has struck its own coins since the early 1790s, after the American Revolution. This book will introduce you to the fun hobby of collecting these interesting and valuable pieces of history.

Silver Siglos of King Croesus of Lydia
This coin was struck sometime between 561 and 546 B.C., by order of King Croesus. Because these had a standard design, standard weight, and official stamp, they are among the first true coins as we define them today. (Actual size approximately 17 mm)

1795 Silver Dollar
This dollar was one of the first coins struck by the United States Mint. Today it's worth thousands of dollars!

COLLECTING COINS

Coins have been around for nearly 3,000 years, which is why many people call coin collecting "the oldest hobby in the world." Today, there are as many as 100 million coin collectors in the United States alone! Many of them started in the hobby by collecting state quarters struck by the U.S. Mint from 1999 to 2008. There are coin shops, clubs, web sites, and conventions where people come from all over the world to buy, sell, trade, make friends, and talk about their hobby.

> A numismatist is a person who collects and studies money. This includes coins and paper currency, and also money-like objects such as tokens and medals. Numismatics is the study of coins and money. This is a popular hobby. More people belong to the American Numismatic Association than the entire population of Juneau, the capital city of Alaska!

Lots of kids collect coins. In fact, the American Numismatic Association (one of the largest coin clubs in the world) has a special group just for "Young Numismatists"–collectors 22 years old or younger.

If you are a Boy Scout, you can earn your Coin Collecting Merit Badge. If you are a Girl Scout, you can earn your "Fun With Money" patch. Junior Girl Scouts can earn a "Collecting Hobbies" badge and Cadette Scouts can earn an interest patch for collecting coins, paper notes, or money-related items.

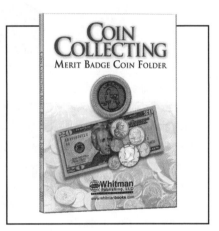

The American Numismatic Association can help you with the information you need to earn your Scout badge or patch. The Outreach Department helps ANA-member leaders conduct a "Coin Collecting Merit Badge Clinic," and the ANA's Young Numismatist (YN) programs provide special collecting information to help you earn your badge.

ANA Merit Badge Clinics are held twice a year, at the ANA National Money Show and the World's Fair of Money. Clinics are also held at ANA Headquarters in Colorado Springs, Colorado. For more information you can email the ANA Outreach Department at outreach@money.org.

THE DIVERSITY OF COINS

Coins come in many shapes and sizes. Most are round, but some are square, rectangular, or even triangular. There are even some coins from Somalia that are shaped like guitars! Some coins are tiny, like the silver three-cent piece made in the United States from 1851 to 1873. That little coin weighs less than a gram–about as much as a single paper clip. A much larger coin is the giant $50 gold commemorative struck in 1915 for the Panama-Pacific Exposition, to celebrate the opening of the Panama Canal. That coin weighs almost 84 grams–it's heavier than three old-fashioned silver dollars!

COINS CAN BE BIG
. . . like this 1915 Panama-Pacific commemorative $50 coin.

And coins can be little
. . . like this tiny silver three-cent piece.

Coins are also made of different metals, including gold, silver, copper, aluminum, brass, steel, bronze, and nickel. You can find coins in strange metals like goloid, zinc, and oroide. Some coins are even made out of two metals! These are called *bimetallic*. Canada has a bimetallic $2 coin. It has a central core made of bronze, which looks golden-brown, and an outer ring made of nickel, which looks silvery.

Coins in ancient times were like newspapers. They spread information throughout a kingdom or empire, and into other lands. Someone looking at a coin would be able to see a king's portrait, or find out about a war or battle commemorated on the coin, or learn about another country's culture and achievements.

French 10-Franc Coin
The design of this French coin is called "Spirit of the Bastille." The central part is made of nickel. The outer ring is mostly copper.

An Ancient Silver Coin From Corinth
Anyone who saw this coin would know it was from Corinth, because it shows Pegasus (the winged horse), who, according to legend, was captured by the Corinthian king.

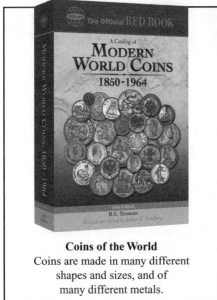

Coins of the World
Coins are made in many different
shapes and sizes, and of
many different metals.

**A Commemorative Coin
From the United States**
This commemorative half
dollar tells everyone who sees
it that in the United States we
value cultural diversity—we're
"A Nation of Immigrants."

Today you can hold a coin that was struck at the Mint this year, or one that was made hundreds of years ago! Think about the history behind these coins. Who knows? An Indian Head cent that was struck in the 1860s might have been in the pocket of young Theodore Roosevelt. A Buffalo nickel from 1937 might have been used by an American soldier to buy a newspaper before he went to fight in Europe during World War II. And a nickel from 2004 shows us what the boat used by explorers Lewis and Clark looked like. Every coin, old or new, has a story to tell. That's part of what makes them fun to collect.

THE PARTS OF A COIN

Obverse? Reverse? Motto? These are some things you'll find on every coin. Once you know the parts of a coin, you'll be able to talk about them with other collectors. Here's a guide to get you started.

Obverse (the Front of the Coin)

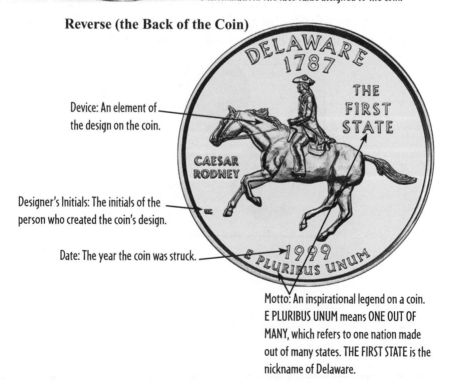

Legend: The principal inscription on a coin.

Edge: The side of the coin.

Rim: The outer, raised portion of the coin.

Field: The flat surface of the coin.

Design: The image on the coin. For example, on this quarter, the design on the obverse is the portrait of President Washington. On the reverse, it is Caesar Rodney riding on horseback.

Mintmark: A letter that tells us which mint struck the coin. For example: P stands for Philadelphia, D for Denver, and S for San Francisco.

Denomination: The *face value* assigned to the coin.

Reverse (the Back of the Coin)

Device: An element of the design on the coin.

Designer's Initials: The initials of the person who created the coin's design.

Date: The year the coin was struck.

Motto: An inspirational legend on a coin. E PLURIBUS UNUM means ONE OUT OF MANY, which refers to one nation made out of many states. THE FIRST STATE is the nickname of Delaware.

How Are Coins Made?

Coins are made by a country's government, which decides how many to make, what kinds to make, what they'll be made of, what they look like, and everything else about them. Most often a coin is designed by an artist who works for the government. Other times, the government will hold a contest so any artist can offer a design. Here are some famous coins that were made by designers who were picked through contests:

Jefferson Nickel

Standing Liberty Quarter

Bicentennial Quarter

Coins are made at a government building called a *mint*. Today, coins are struck by the U.S. Mint in Philadelphia and at three "branch mints," in Denver, San Francisco, and West Point. You can tell where a coin was struck by its *mintmark*–a little letter stamped on the coin (P for Philadelphia, D for Denver, S for San Francisco, W for West Point).

In the past, coins were also struck at mints in other cities. Here is a list of every U.S. mint location and their mintmarks. Do you know which states they're located in? (The answers are on the next page.)

Mintmark	Which State?
C = Charlotte	_____
CC = Carson City	_____
D = Dahlonega (for gold coins)	_____
D = Denver	_____
O = New Orleans	_____
P = Philadelphia	_____
S = San Francisco	_____
W = West Point	_____

Stump Your Friends!

There was another mint that was run by the U.S. government—but not in the United States! The U.S. operated a mint in Manila, the capital city of the Philippines, from 1920 through 1941, when the islands were an American possession.

Some Philippine Coins
These are some of the coins struck in Manila by the government of the United States.

Modern-Day Mintmarks

Today, you can find P and D mintmarks on coins in your pocket change.

The San Francisco Mint as it appeared in 1874 when it was ready to be used for coinage.
(Banker's Almanac)

The first Philadelphia Mint. Erected in 1792, it remained in use continuously through 1832.

Where Are the Mints Located?

Charlotte is in North Carolina. Carson City is in Nevada. Dahlonega is in Georgia. Denver is in Colorado. New Orleans is in Louisiana. Philadelphia is in Pennsylvania. San Francisco is in California. West Point is in New York.

If you answered all eight correctly, you're a numismatic superstar. Ask a grownup and see if they can get them all right!

TYPES OF U.S. MINT COINS

The U.S. Mint makes several kinds of coins.

Circulation Strikes

Circulation strikes are regular coins that people use to buy and sell things. The Mint makes billions of these coins every year. Each coin is struck in a big machine called a *press*, and then dumped into a bin with thousands of other coins of the same denomination. Then they're counted, put into bags, and sent out to banks for distribution. The coins aren't handled very carefully, because they're made for business, not for collecting. The idea is to make lots of them as quickly as possible.

Steam-Powered Press, Used Starting in 1836
This machine could make 40,000 coins per day. Before that, the Mint's old hand-operated screw-action presses could only make 13,000 coins per day. Today the Philadelphia Mint can make *32 million* coins in a single day. Running full-time, it would take this steam-powered press more than two years to make that many coins, assuming it didn't break down first!

Mint Set Coins

Every year, the Mint makes some coins especially for collectors, and puts them into special packages as *Mint sets*. Each Mint set has one example of each denomination and design from each mint that made coins that year.

For example, the 2009 Mint sets have four Lincoln Bicentennial cents, one nickel, one dime, one each of the six quarters for that year, one half dollar, four Presidential dollars, and one Native American dollar from Philadelphia, plus

2009 Mint Set

the same number of each coin from Denver. That's a total of 36 coins. These coins are made like normal circulation strikes, but after they are struck, they are placed into the sets instead of being dumped into bins with other coins.

Proof Set Coins

Every year, the Mint also makes *Proof* coins for collectors. These coins use the same designs as circulation strikes, but they're made from special dies that are polished to give the coins reflective surfaces like mirrors. The dies are cleaned often (after every 15 to 25 impressions), and are replaced frequently so they don't wear out. The coin *blanks* (pieces of metal the Proof coins are struck from) are also cleaned and polished to assure quality. Proof coins are struck at high pressure and slow speed, two or more times per coin. Each finished Proof coin is individually inspected, and handled carefully with gloves or tongs. They also get a final inspection by packers before being sonically sealed into special plastic cases.

The end result? Beautiful, flawless examples of America's coins–numismatic perfection!

Commemorative Coins

Commemorative coins have been popular since the days of the Greeks and Romans. In the beginning they recorded and honored important events and people. There were no newspapers back then, and commemorative coins were useful in passing along news of the day.

Many modern nations have issued commemorative coins, and numismatists enjoy collecting them. Many American collectors feel the commemoratives of the United States are the most beautiful in the world. Collectors in other countries might feel the same way about *their* commemoratives!

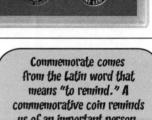

Commemorate comes from the Latin word that means "to remind." A commemorative coin reminds us of an important person, place, or event.

A British Commemorative Coin
This silver crown was struck in 1935 to celebrate George V's 25th year as king of Great Britain. St. George on horseback, slaying a dragon, is an ancient British image, but here it's given a modern, stylish look— collectors call it the "Rocking Horse crown."

An American Commemorative Coin
This U.S. half dollar from 1936 honors the Civil War soldiers—from both North and South—who fought in the Battle of Gettysburg.

How Much Is a Coin Worth?

How much is a half dollar worth? That might be a trick question. A coin can have several kinds of value. A quarter dollar might be worth a lot more than 25 cents!

Every coin has a *face value*, or *denomination*. This is how much the coin is worth as spending money. For example, the face value of a half dollar is fifty cents, enough to buy a couple big gumballs in the machine at the supermarket. A coin's face value is guaranteed by the federal government. You will *always* be able to spend a half dollar for fifty cents!

A coin can also have *intrinsic value*. This is the value of the metal that makes up the coin—how much it would be worth if you melted it down. A modern half dollar is made of copper and nickel, two inexpensive metals. The coin's intrinsic value is maybe ten cents. An older half dollar is made out of silver, a much more valuable metal. If silver is worth $18 an ounce, the older half dollar has an intrinsic value of $6.51.

A third kind of value a coin can have is its *numismatic value*. This is how much it's worth to a coin collector. Numismatic value depends on how rare the coin is, the condition it's in (called its *grade*), how many people like to collect it, and other factors.

Older *Silver* Half Dollar

Modern *Copper-Nickel* Half Dollar

1897 Barber Half Dollar
2,480,000 Barber half dollars were struck at the Philadelphia Mint in 1897. That means this coin is old and somewhat uncommon. In Mint State (with no traces of wear or damage), its numismatic value is $500 or more.

1952 Franklin Half Dollar
More than 21 million Franklin half dollars were struck in 1952. That's a lot of coins! Because this one is fairly common, its numismatic value is about $20 in Mint State.

How to Examine Your Coins

You should always handle rare coins carefully. Even though they're made of metal, they can be damaged by dirt, or dropping, or moisture, or other factors. Here are some guidelines on proper handling, lighting, and magnification.

Proper Handling

1. Examine your coin over a soft surface, so it doesn't get damaged if you accidentally drop it. Always handle a coin by the edge, held between your fingertips. Never touch its surface. Oil, acid, and dirt from your fingertips can damage a coin and leave ugly fingerprints. This will lower your coin's value. Some collectors wear cotton gloves when they examine their coins, especially higher-grade examples. With proper care, your bare fingers should be fine.

2. Do not hold a coin near your mouth while you talk. Small drops of moisture that land on the coin's surface can cause spots on the surface.

3. To study your coin, hold it at an angle, so that light from the bulb above reflects from the coin's surface into your eye. Turn and rotate the coin so you can observe its details from all angles. You should also examine the edge.

4. You will find that scratches or *hairlines* that are visible at one angle may become invisible when the coin is rotated. Take your time. Don't be in a hurry. Enjoy the beauty of your coin.

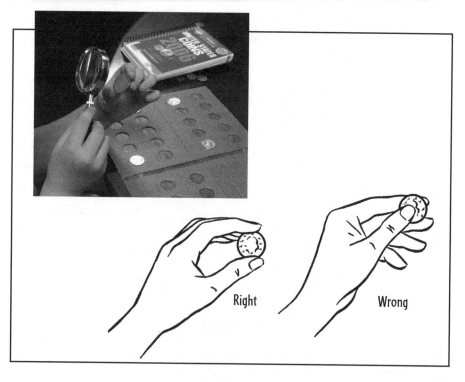

Right   Wrong

PROPER LIGHTING

Viewed under five different lighting conditions, a single coin can have five completely different appearances. Use a strong lamp light to observe your coins. Look at them in an area free of light from sources other than your lamp.

PROPER MAGNIFICATION

As with lighting, proper magnification can reveal much about a coin, including flaws that are hidden to the naked eye. Use a magnifying glass of at least three power (3x) and up to eight power (8x) strength or more. This will reveal scratches and other marks.

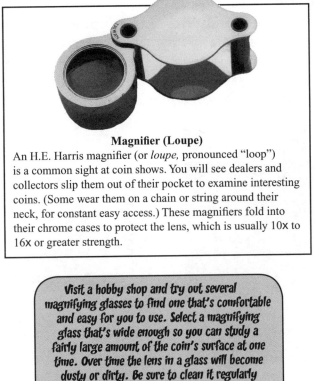

Magnifier (Loupe)

An H.E. Harris magnifier (or *loupe,* pronounced "loop") is a common sight at coin shows. You will see dealers and collectors slip them out of their pocket to examine interesting coins. (Some wear them on a chain or string around their neck, for constant easy access.) These magnifiers fold into their chrome cases to protect the lens, which is usually 10x to 16x or greater strength.

> Visit a hobby shop and try out several magnifying glasses to find one that's comfortable and easy for you to use. Select a magnifying glass that's wide enough so you can study a fairly large amount of the coin's surface at one time. Over time the lens in a glass will become dusty or dirty. Be sure to clean it regularly (being careful not to injure the surface).

How to Grade Your Coins

n the sixth edition of the *Official American Numismatic Association Grading Standards for United States Coins*, numismatist Kenneth Bressett says:

> Grading is really very simple. All you need is four things:
> 1. A good magnifying glass,
> 2. A good light,
> 3. A good memory, and
> 4. 20 years of experience.

It's a good thing Mr. Bressett was just joking—or only grownups would be able to grade coins!

Getting Started

Obviously, you shouldn't have to wait 20 years before you jump into coin collecting. One of the best ways to learn about coins in general is by reading—and you're off to a good start with this book. After this, you can read a beginner's book devoted to grading, such as *The Whitman Insider Guide to Grading United States Coins*. When you're ready for a more advanced book, you can look into the *Official ANA Grading Standards* or *Grading Coins by Photographs: An Action Guide for the Collector and Investor*. These guides

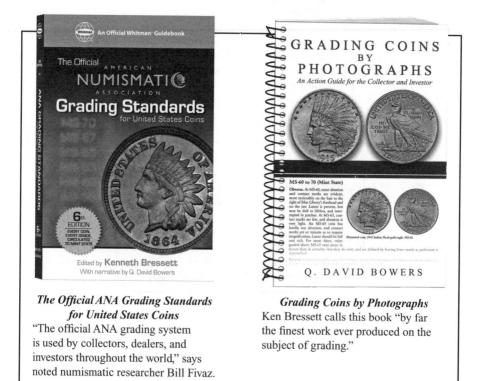

The Official ANA Grading Standards for United States Coins
"The official ANA grading system is used by collectors, dealers, and investors throughout the world," says noted numismatic researcher Bill Fivaz.

Grading Coins by Photographs
Ken Bressett calls this book "by far the finest work ever produced on the subject of grading."

show photographs of a coin in a particular grade, with a text description of its appearance in that grade. By reading the text and comparing your coin to the photos, you will be able to confidently grade your coin.

When it comes to grading coins, the more you look at, the better. This will make you familiar with how coins look in different conditions.

PRACTICE, PRACTICE, PRACTICE

Reach into your pocket and take out the coins you have there. Or dump out your piggy bank. Or ask your mom or dad to go to a local bank and buy a few wrapped rolls of common modern coins–cents, nickels, dimes, quarters, or dollars.

Now, examine these coins carefully. You will see some in bright Mint State, with very few marks, as well as some older coins that are well worn. By looking at hundreds of modern coins, you will see differences in mint luster, strike, and other grading factors. Think of this as a free education–you can always spend your "class materials" when you're done with them!

Once you've had some practice with common modern coins, you can concentrate on a single older series or type, such as Lincoln wheat cents, Morgan silver dollars, or Buffalo nickels. Go to a coin show and examine every Buffalo nickel you can, from low-grade, worn examples to high-grade coins with bright luster. Ask questions. Soon, from this "field work," you'll have a good feel for the series.

These photographs show Buffalo nickels in three grades (out of a possible 70): MS-65, EF-45, and AG-3. You'll find more on these letter-and-number abbreviations in the next chapter.

Buffalo Nickel in Mint State
In Mint State, a Buffalo nickel has no trace of wear, though it may have slight blemishes such as hard-to-see nicks. The details in the Indian's portrait and the bison are sharp and complete. In higher grades of Mint State, it will have its original mint luster.

Buffalo Nickel in Extremely Fine Condition
In Extremely Fine condition, a Buffalo nickel shows slight wear on the hair above the braid, the temple, and the hair near the cheekbone. On the reverse, the high points of the bison's hip and thigh are lightly worn. The horn is sharp and nearly complete.

Buffalo Nickel in About Good Condition
In About Good condition, a Buffalo nickel is very worn, with parts of the date, legend, and details worn smooth. The design is outlined. The letters will merge into the coin's rims. This is a nickel that saw a lot of hand-to-hand circulation!

GRADING TERMINOLOGY

A non-collector might assume a description of "Good" means a coin is well preserved and very desirable. However, a numismatist knows that "Good" is one of the lowest grades, and that a coin in this condition is well worn, with most of its details gone.

Exactly how much wear does the coin have? How many marks or dings are on its surface? Does it have any of its original mint luster? These are questions that coin collectors think about when they grade coins. The ANA uses a 70-point grading system, where 70 is perfection, and 1 is the worst condition.

PROOF COIN GRADES

Proof refers to the way a coin is made, and is not a grade itself. A Proof is a special coin made at the Mint as a souvenir or collectible. These are classified from PF-70 (perfection) down to PF-60. Three typical levels of Proof:

PF-65–A Proof-65 coin (abbreviated as PF-65, and sometimes called *gem Proof*) has brilliant surfaces with no noticeable blemishes or flaws. It may have a few scattered, barely noticeable marks or hairlines.

PF-63–A Proof-63 coin (abbreviated as PF-63, and sometimes called *choice Proof*) has reflective surfaces with only a few blemishes in secondary focal places. It has no major flaws.

PF-60–A Proof-60 coin (abbreviated as PF-60, with no special adjective) may have a surface with several contact marks, hairlines, or light rubs. Its surface may be dull and it might lack eye appeal.

CIRCULATION-STRIKE COIN GRADES

A circulation-strike coin is any coin minted for commerce. These start out in Mint State at the moment they're pushed from the coinage press. Another word for Mint State is Uncirculated (abbreviated as Unc.). Gradually a coin will wear down, as it is spent from hand to hand, to About Good condition.

Commonly encountered grading levels on the ANA's 70-point grading scale:

MS-70–An MS-70 coin (sometimes described as *Perfect Uncirculated*) is in perfect new condition, showing no trace of wear. This is the finest possible quality, with no scratches or marks. Very few regular-issue coins are ever found in this condition.

MS-65–An MS-65 coin (often described as *Gem Uncirculated*) is an above-average Uncirculated example. It might be brilliant or lightly toned, and has very few contact marks on the surface or rim. MS-67 through MS-62 indicate slightly higher or lower grades of preservation.

MS-63–An MS-63 coin (often described as *Choice Uncirculated*) has some distracting contact marks or blemishes in prime focal areas. Its luster might not be as nice as a higher-grade coin.

MS-60–An MS-60 coin (typically described simply as *Uncirculated* or *Mint State*) has no trace of wear, but may show a number of contact marks. Its surface may be spotted or lack some luster.

AU-55–An AU-55 coin (*Choice About Uncirculated*, in the ANA's words) has evidence of rubbing on the high points of its design. Most of its mint luster remains.

AU-50–An AU-50 coin (*About Uncirculated*) has traces of light wear on many of its high points. At least half of the mint luster is still present.

EF-45–An EF-45 coin (*Choice Extremely Fine*) has light overall wear on its highest points. All design details are very sharp. Some of the mint luster is evident.

EF-40–An EF-40 coin (*Extremely Fine*) has light wear throughout the design, but all its features are sharp and well defined. Traces of luster may show.

VF-30–A VF-30 coin (*Choice Very Fine*) has light, even wear on the surface and highest parts of its design. All of its lettering and major features are sharp.

VF-20–A VF-20 coin (*Very Fine*) has moderate wear on the high points of its design. All major details are clear.

F-12–An F-12 coin (*Fine*) has moderate to considerable even wear. Its entire design is bold with an overall pleasing appearance.

VG-8–A VG-8 coin (*Very Good*) is well worn, with its main features clear and bold, although rather flat.

G-4–A G-4 coin (*Good*) is heavily worn, with its design visible but faint in areas. Many details are flat.

AG-3–An AG-3 coin (*About Good*) is very heavily worn, with portions of its lettering, date, and legend worn smooth. The date may be barely readable.

**Morgan Dollar
in Mint State**

**Morgan Dollar
in Good Condition**

A PHOTO GUIDE TO GRADING

This chapter shows you how to grade one of the most popular United States coin series: Liberty Walking half dollars, struck from 1916 to 1947. Study the photos, read the descriptions, and, if you own an example of this coin, compare it to what you see here. Soon you will have a good understanding of what to look for as you grade.

MINT STATE

A Mint State Liberty Walking half dollar has no trace of wear.

MS-70– A flawless coin exactly as it was minted, with no trace of wear or damage. Must have full mint luster and brilliance or light toning.

MS-67– Almost flawless, but with very minor problems.

MS-65– No trace of wear; nearly as perfect as MS-67 except for some small blemishes. Has full mint luster but may be unevenly toned or have light fingerprints. May be weakly struck in one or two small spots. May have a few tiny nicks or marks.

MS-63– A Mint State coin with attractive mint luster, but noticeable contact marks or minor blemishes.

MS-60– An Uncirculated coin with no trace of wear, but with blemishes more obvious than for MS-63. May lack full mint luster, and surface may be dull, spotted, or heavily toned. A few small spots may be weakly struck.

ABOUT UNCIRCULATED

An About Uncirculated Liberty Walking half dollar has small traces of wear visible on its highest design points.

AU-58 (Very Choice AU)–Has some signs of rubbing. On the obverse, check the hair above Liberty's temple, the right arm, and the left breast. On the reverse, check the high points of the eagle's head, breast, legs, and wings.

AU-55 (Choice AU)–Much of the mint luster is still present, but often lightly worn in the obverse right field. The obverse shows only a trace of wear on the highest points of the head, breast, and right arm. The reverse shows a trace of wear below the eagle's neck, and on the left leg between the breast and left wing.

AU-50–Some mint luster is still present. The obverse shows traces of wear on the head, breast, arms, and left leg. The reverse shows traces of wear on high points of the wings and at the center of the head. All leg feathers are visible.

EXTREMELY FINE

An Extremely Fine Liberty Walking half dollar has very light wear on only its highest design points.

EF-45 (Choice)–Part of the mint luster is still present. The obverse shows light wear spots on the head, breast, arms, left leg, and foot. Nearly all gown lines are clearly visible. Sandal details are bold and complete. The knee is lightly worn but full and rounded. On the reverse, small flat spots show on high points of the eagle's breast and legs. The wing feathers have nearly full details.

EF-40–Traces of mint luster may still show. On the obverse, wear shows on the head, breast, arms, and left leg. Nearly all gown lines are visible. Sandal details are complete. The breast and knee are nearly flat. On the reverse, the high points of the eagle are lightly worn. Half the breast and leg feathers are visible. Central parts of the feathers below the neck are well worn.

VERY FINE

A Very Fine Liberty Walking half dollar has light to moderate even wear. All major features are sharp.

VF-30 (Choice)–On the obverse, wear spots show on the head, breast, arms, and legs. The left leg is rounded but worn from above the knee to the ankle. The gown line crossing the body is partially visible. The knee is flat. The outline of the breast can be seen. On the reverse, the breast and legs of the eagle are moderately worn but clearly separated, with some feathers visible between them. The feather ends and folds are clearly visible in the right wing. The pupil of the eye is visible.

VF-20–On the obverse, the left leg is worn nearly flat. Wear spots show on the head, breast, arms, and foot. The breast is outlined. On the reverse, the entire eagle is lightly worn, but most major details are visible. The breast, central part of the legs, and top edge of the right wing are worn flat.

FINE

A Fine Liberty Walking half dollar has moderate to heavy even wear. Its entire design is clear and bold.

F-12–On the obverse, the gown stripes are worn but show clearly (except for pre-1921 coins, on which only half are visible). The right leg is lightly worn. The left leg is nearly flat and the sandal is worn but visible. The center of the body is worn, but some of the gown is visible. On the reverse, the breast is worn smooth. Half the wing feathers are visible although well worn in spots. The top two layers of feathers are visible in the left wing. The rim is full.

Very Good

A Very Good Liberty Walking half dollar is well worn. Its design is clear but flat and lacking details.

VG-8–On the obverse, the entire design is weak. Most details in the gown are worn smooth (except for coins after 1921, on which half the stripes must show). The date and all letters are clear, but the top of the motto may be weak. The rim is complete. The drapery across the body is partially visible. On the reverse, about one third of the feathers are visible, and the large feathers at the ends of the wings are well separated. The eagle's eye is visible. The rim is full and all letters are clear.

Good

A Good Liberty Walking half dollar is heavily worn. Its design and legend are visible but faint in spots.

G-4–On the obverse, the entire design is well worn, with very little detail remaining. The legend and date are weak but visible. The top of the date may be worn flat. The rim is flat but nearly complete. On the reverse, the eagle is worn nearly flat but is completely outlined. The lettering and motto are worn but clearly visible.

About Good

An About Good Liberty Walking half dollar shows only the outline of its design. Parts of the date and legend are worn smooth.

AG-3–On the obverse, the figure of Miss Liberty is outlined, with nearly all details worn away. The legend is visible but half worn away. The date is weak but readable. The rim merges with the lettering. On the reverse, the entire design is partially worn away. The letters merge with the rim.

BUYING COINS

One of the oldest and best ways of starting a coin collection is by picking coins from circulation–the ones you get in pocket change. For example, you will be able to find most of the National Park quarters in change, or from coins your mom or dad bring home. If you need a certain National Park quarter and a friend has two of them, maybe he'll trade you one for another in *your* collection! (Remember how people used to *barter,* like the vegetable farmer who wanted a goat, in this book's introduction?) The best part about collecting coins from circulation is that they only cost you their face value.

Do you have a friend or relative who is going to another country for vacation or business? You might ask them to bring back a few coins for your collection!

Most rare coins aren't easy to find in pocket change. To collect them, you will have to buy them at a coin shop, from the U.S. Mint, at a coin show, through the mail, or someplace else. (Or you might get them as presents from relatives and friends who know you collect coins.) Before you start buying coins, learn about them by reading a book or two. For United States coins, the *Guide Book of United States Coins,* often called the "Red Book," is a good place to start. It tells about every U.S. coin minted since colonial times.

By reading about a coin–how rare it is, how to grade it, how much it's worth in different grades– you will have a good start for when you start looking to buy.

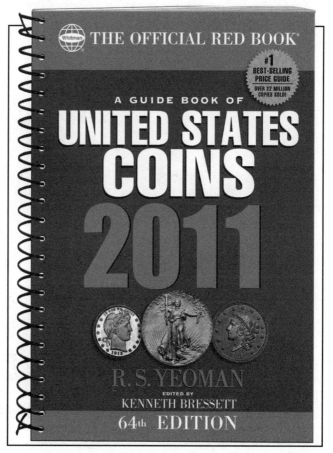

STORING YOUR COINS

Your coins are valuable, even if they're only worth face value. It's important to protect them and store them correctly so they don't get damaged. You can store them in ways that will display them, so your friends and family can see them and learn about them. Some of the ways to store your coins include folders, albums, cardboard holders, and hard plastic holders. As always, handle them carefully when you store them.

Folders

There are many coin folders for storing your collection. People have been putting their coins in folders for almost a hundred years; it's a very popular way to store and display them. If you go to a coin shop, bookstore, or hobby shop, you will find folders for every kind of U.S. coin, from copper half cents to gold pieces.

Each folder has openings where you can insert your coins–one for each date and mintmark. The idea is to fill each opening as you find (or buy) more coins for your collection, and after a while you'll have the entire folder filled up! This can take many weeks, months, or even years. The challenge of finding one of every date is part of the fun of collecting.

Some folders are fancy, like these map folders for National Park quarters. They have information about each park, plus illustrations and a map of the whole country. These are a good way to display your collection, and you can easily see which coins you still need.

Coin folders are a durable and attractive way to store your collection, and most of them cost only a few dollars each.

Albums

With a *folder*, you can only see one side of each coin–the side facing out. With an *album*, you can see both sides. Coin albums look like fancy books that you can keep your collection in. They have removable plastic slides that protect both sides of your coins.

CARDBOARD HOLDERS

At a coin show, you will often see coins in 2"x2" cardboard holders with clear windows. These are an inexpensive, easy way to store your coins and protect them from dust, fingerprints, and other things that can damage them.

The 2"x2" cardboard holders (often called *two-by-twos*) have windows of different sizes for different coins. Place your coin in the middle, fold it over, and then staple all four sides. Now you can look at both sides of your coin. You can write on the cardboard (the year of the coin, its grade, how much you paid for it, who you bought it from, etc.).

Coins in 2"x2" cardboard holders are easy to store in boxes. In fact, you can buy long cardboard boxes made just for storing them. You can also buy vinyl pages that have special sleeves for holding 2"x2" cardboard holders. These fit into a three-ring binder so you can look at your collection like a book.

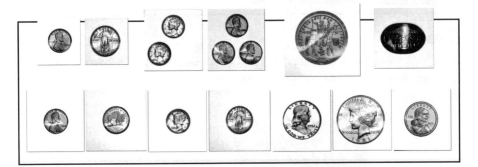

HARD PLASTIC HOLDERS

The best protection for your coins comes from hard plastic holders. These usually measure 2"x2", like a cardboard holder, and are big enough for a single coin. Some are longer, with openings for several coins. You put your coin in the opening in the middle and then click the two plastic halves together to hold it.

Another kind of plastic holder is a coin *tube*. These are clear or frosty holders that store a certain number of coins of a particular type—for example, 40 quarters, or 40 nickels, or 50 cents.

STORAGE TIPS FOR YOUR COINS

You should store your coins in a dry place. Dampness can make them oxidize (like rust) or, in extreme cases, corrode.

Avoid dampness by moving your coins to a drier location. If this is not possible, then put a packet of silica gel (available in drugstores or photography supply shops) in with the coins, and replace it regularly. This will absorb moisture. Also, storing your coins in airtight containers will help.

The more a coin is exposed to freely circulating air, the more likely it is to change color or to tone. Storing your coins in protective envelopes and hard plastic holders will usually (but not always) help prevent this.

Do not buy any coin storage containers unless you know what they're made of. A few years ago clear flexible plastic envelopes or "flips" were very popular for storing coins. These were made of a plastic called PVC. Some coin albums were made of this material as well. Over time, PVC can form a harmful goo that damages the surfaces of your coins.

Another important tip related to storing and preserving your collection: even if a coin is dirty or toned, you should not try to clean it. Cleaning with polishes, pastes, or other chemicals can strip a coin of its natural luster. This will make it less valuable.

COLLECTING NATIONAL PARK QUARTERS

National park quarters: since these new coins were announced in 2009, everybody has been talking about them!

Like the very popular state quarters of 1999 to 2008, and the District of Columbia and territorial quarters of 2009, the national park quarters have captured the attention and interest of just about every coin collector. Millions of people–some who consider themselves serious numismatists, and others who just like to collect these neat coins–eagerly check their pocket change to see what's new, to find a coin honoring the Grand Canyon, Hot Springs, Yosemite, or other favorite national parks, or to see the latest designs.

Each year since 2010 the U.S. Mint has issued five new designs, each featuring a different national park or other national site, in the order in which they were established. In the pages to follow you will learn all about these fascinating coins–remarkable in their diversity, unequalled in their historical importance, and inexpensive enough that anyone can afford to collect them.

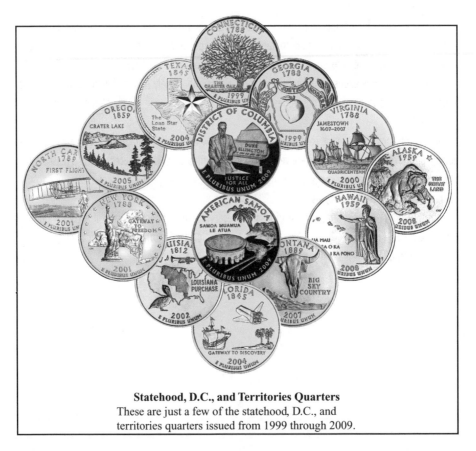

Statehood, D.C., and Territories Quarters
These are just a few of the statehood, D.C., and
territories quarters issued from 1999 through 2009.

Basic Facts (for All National Park Quarters, 2010-2021)

Designer. The first obverse portrait of George Washington was designed by John Flanagan for the 1932 quarter (his initials, JF, were placed on the president's neck). The portrait was changed in 1999 by William Cousins, who added more detail in the hair. Cousins's initials, WC, were added to those of Flanagan, run together as JFWC. This portrait was used for the state, D.C., and territorial quarters (1999–2009). For the national park quarters the portrait was changed again, to be closer in appearance to Flanagan's original design. When it comes to the *reverses,* many different designers and Mint engravers are involved.

Obverse and Reverse. The national park quarter obverse is the same for every coin in the series, except for the date change every year. This design is different from the quarters of 1932 to 1998. To make room for the creative designs on the reverse, the inscriptions UNITED STATES OF AMERICA and QUARTER DOLLAR were relocated to the obverse, above and below the portrait. LIBERTY and IN GOD WE TRUST were moved to new positions. As noted above, the George Washington portrait used on national park quarters is different from the one used on the state, D.C., and territorial quarters.

Specifications (Clad Issues). *Composition:* Outer layers of copper-nickel (75% copper and 25% nickel) bonded to an inner core of pure copper. The copper is visible by viewing the coin edge-on. • *Diameter:* 24.3 mm • *Weight:* 5.67 grams • *Edge:* Reeded.

Specifications (Silver Issues). *Composition:* 90% silver; 10% copper • *Diameter:* 24.3 mm • *Weight:* 6.25 grams • *Edge:* Reeded.

**Compare the Three Designs (1932 Quarter,
Statehood Quarter, and National Park Quarter)**
How many differences can you see?

2010 ARKANSAS
HOT SPRINGS NATIONAL PARK

April 20, 1832

V isitors come from all over to enjoy the beautiful historic buildings at Hot Springs National Park. Even before the bath houses were built, though, people valued the area for its warm, bubbling waters. They believed these hot baths, rich with minerals, could cure aches and pains.

President Thomas Jefferson sent explorers to learn more about the springs in 1804. Soon Americans knew that we had an important resource here. In 1832 President Andrew Jackson made Hot Springs the very first park protected by our federal government. You can visit today, and see the amazing natural sights that Americans have enjoyed for more than 200 years.

The water that rises from the ground here is steaming hot— and more than 4,000 years old!

HOT SPRINGS, ARKANSAS

2010 WYOMING
YELLOWSTONE NATIONAL PARK

March 1, 1872

There are more than 10,000 smoking, bubbling, hot-water springs and other thermal features in Yellowstone National Park. You can see the tallest geyser in the world here–it's called Steamboat, and it's one of 300 of these hot, explosive fountains. You may have heard of another famous geyser in Yellowstone: Old Faithful, which shoots water and steam high into the air about every 90 minutes. When American explorers told people back home about these marvelous sights, not everybody believed them!

By the early 1870s, scientists had studied and photographed the park's wonders. In 1872 President Ulysses S. Grant made Yellowstone an official *national park*–the first in the world. Other countries saw the wisdom in protecting and caring for such unique natural places, and they started to set aside national parks of their own.

If you like to play outdoors, Yellowstone has 2.2 million acres to explore, and more than 1,100 miles of hiking trails. And if you like animals, watch for wolves, bison, elk, bears, and others who call Yellowstone home.

This landscape was the first-ever U.S. national park, managed and preserved by the federal government for everyone to enjoy.

YELLOWSTONE NATIONAL PARK, WYOMING

2010
CALIFORNIA
YOSEMITE NATIONAL PARK

October 1, 1890

The Yosemite Valley, wrote John Muir in 1912, "looks like an immense hall or temple lighted from above." The famous naturalist first visited the area in 1868. A few years earlier, President Abraham Lincoln had given the valley and the giant redwood trees in nearby Mariposa Grove to the state of California, for preservation. With inspiring landmarks like El Capitan (a 300-story-tall rock formation), the legendary Bridalveil Fall (whose mist is supposed to increase your chance of marriage), and majestic Half Dome (a granite block nearly a mile tall), Americans knew they had something special. In 1890 the region was protected as Yosemite National Park.

Every year more than 3.5 million visitors explore the park's valleys and peaks. They're rewarded with amazing views that impressed John Muir, famous photographer Ansel Adams, and millions of other Americans who love nature.

NATIONAL PARK QUARTERS

YOSEMITE, CALIFORNIA

The giant sequoia trees in Yosemite are the largest of all living things on earth.

2010
ARIZONA
GRAND CANYON NATIONAL PARK

February 20, 1893

It's hard to describe Grand Canyon National Park with words—you have to visit it in person to truly experience its power, color, and beauty. America's great landscape painters and photographers have tried to capture it. When you visit, you can decide if they were successful.

Native Americans occupied the canyon for centuries—the Anasazi, the Cohonina, the Paiutes, the Cerbat, and the Navajo all knew of it. By the late 1800s it was a tourist destination. Visitors came by stagecoach, then by train, and later by car, to see the 4,000-foot-deep gorge. In 1893 it received federal protection. In 1908, President Theodore Roosevelt made it a national monument, and in 1919 it became a national park.

In 1919, more than 40,000 tourists visited the Grand Canyon. This year, about 5 *million* will! You can see the canyon from a boat on the Colorado River, or by floating in a big raft, or by riding a mule on the rocky paths.

In the Grand Canyon, the Colorado River carved through layers of rock that took more than a billion years to form.

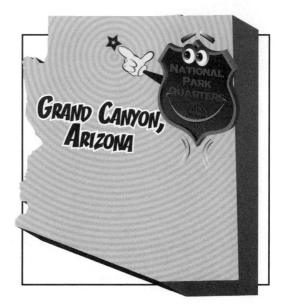

GRAND CANYON, ARIZONA

2010 OREGON
MT. HOOD NATIONAL FOREST

September 28, 1893

In *America's Beautiful National Parks: Collecting the New National Park Quarters*, Aaron McKeon says, "Mt. Hood National Forest in northwestern Oregon is Portland's playground, complete with a splash park (the Clackamas River), plenty of space for picnics (124,000 acres of wilderness area), and a large climbing area."

The forest includes more than a million acres of land and 150 lakes and ponds stocked with fish. You can go whitewater rafting, skiing, hiking, snowboarding, and camping there. Experienced mountain climbers start at the famous Timberline Lodge and make their way up, up, up–about 11,000 feet to the top of Mt. Hood! That's more than two miles of mountain climbing. On flatter ground, hikers enjoy hundreds of miles of trails, including some of the best nature paths in the state of Oregon.

Mt. Hood is the second-most-climbed mountain in the world.

SANDY, OREGON

2011 PENNSYLVANIA
GETTYSBURG NATIONAL MILITARY PARK

February 11, 1895

The Battle of Gettysburg in July 1863 was the turning point in America's long, bloody Civil War. Some 170,000 soldiers fought there. Nearly one out of every three would end up dead, injured, or missing in action. It was a turning point because after the battle the Confederacy lost steam, and General Robert E. Lee was unable to invade the North. That November, President Abraham Lincoln gave a famous speech known as the Gettysburg Address. Lincoln said that the soldiers died for one of the best possible causes—to save the nation.

Today Gettysburg National Military Park honors the soldiers from both sides of the battle. Many Americans believe it to be sacred land: not just orchards, hills, and fields, but a place that saw the destiny of the United States unfold. For that reason, it was made a national park in February 1895.

Every year in July, thousands of history buffs from around the world come here to reenact the Battle of Gettysburg.

GETTYSBURG, PENNSYLVANIA

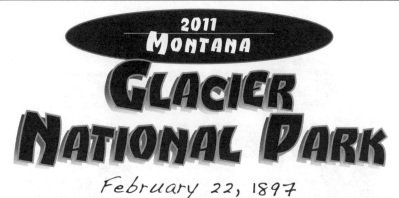

2011
MONTANA
GLACIER NATIONAL PARK

February 22, 1897

Glacier National Park is one of the wildest parks in the continental United States, far away from civilization in the Rocky Mountain wilderness. It's a place where you can see waterfalls and look out for grizzly bears. You can also hike 700 miles of trails, explore on a guided horseback ride, take a boat out on the lakes, go camping, and watch for bobcats, lynx, mountain lions, coyotes, bighorn sheep, mountain goats, and other wild animals.

This remote park was started in the late 1800s. The owners of the Great Northern Railway thought that they'd get more travelers if the land around their railroad was protected by the government and promoted as a tourist destination. They were right. Now, more than a hundred years later, Americans and other nature lovers still come to Glacier National Park knowing they're in for a unique outdoor adventure.

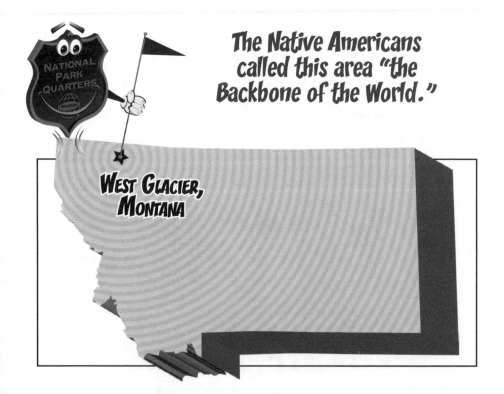

The Native Americans called this area "the Backbone of the World."

WEST GLACIER, MONTANA

2011 WASHINGTON
OLYMPIC NATIONAL PARK

February 22, 1897

Hundreds of adventures await you in Olympic National Park in western Washington, with rain forests to explore, not to mention lakes, waterfalls, mountain trails, glaciers, and coastline. Don't forget to take your camera, because you can see Roosevelt elk, cougars, bears, and bobcats. Not far from the shore, you might spot whales, sea lions, dolphins, and other exotic animals. If you lived in the park 12,000 years ago, you would have seen large elephant-like animals called *mastodons* bending tree branches down with their trunks so they could eat the leaves.

At Olympic National Park, outdoor activity doesn't end in the summer or fall. In the winter you can go skiing, snowshoeing, and sledding. Some animals hibernate, but others stick around throughout the cold months. If you're lucky, you might see a snowshoe hare running around outside, even though there's ten feet of snow on the ground!

Rain forests aren't just in the tropics—this one is near the northern border of the continental United States.

NATIONAL PARK QUARTERS

PORT ANGELES, WASHINGTON

2011 MISSISSIPPI VICKSBURG NATIONAL MILITARY PARK

February 21, 1899

Vicksburg was one of the most important Southern cities of the American Civil War. It wasn't the capital of the Confederacy... it didn't have a mint for striking gold and silver into coins... and it wasn't where President Jefferson Davis lived. But it was located on the Mississippi River–and if you controlled the Mississippi, you controlled the biggest "highway" stretching from North to South. Union soldiers, guns, food, and military supplies couldn't move up and down the river as long as the Confederates were in charge in Vicksburg. The flow was blocked from other cities on the Mississippi, like Minneapolis, St. Paul, Davenport, St. Louis, Memphis, Baton Rouge, and New Orleans.

General Ulysses S. Grant was finally able to capture Vicksburg after months of trying. The way he took over the well-defended fortifications was by a siege–digging in his artillery, bombarding with shells, and keeping food and fresh supplies from entering the city. Within six weeks, with Vicksburg's 30,000 soldiers and 5,000 citizens starving, hungry enough to literally eat a horse, Confederate general John Pemberton surrendered. Along with the Battle of Gettysburg, many historians consider the surrender of Vicksburg to be a turning point of the war. Now the North controlled the Mississippi. "The Father of Waters," wrote Abraham Lincoln, "again goes unvexed to the sea."

The USS *Cairo*, displayed in the park, was the first U.S. ship to be sunk by a mine, on December 12, 1862.

VICKSBURG, MISSISSIPPI

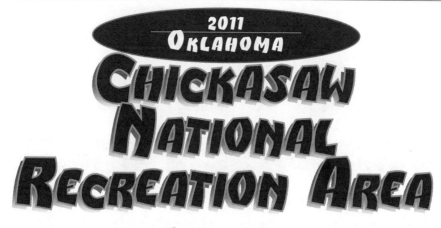

2011
OKLAHOMA
CHICKASAW NATIONAL RECREATION AREA

July 1, 1902

The 10,000-acre Chickasaw National Recreation Area has a long history as an Indian reservation and a pioneer community. White settlers traveling west discovered mineral springs where two creeks came together, and built the small village of Sulphur, naming it for the pungent, sulfurous water, which was thought to cure sickness. The Chickasaw Indians agreed with the white residents that the region's natural resources should be protected, and they sold 640 acres of land to the federal government in 1902. This national site is named in honor of the people of the Chickasaw Nation.

Between 1917 and 1925 a small zoo was kept here, including deer, elk, bison, ostriches, and a bald eagle.

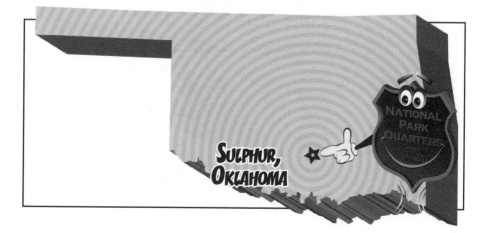

SULPHUR, OKLAHOMA

NATIONAL PARK QUARTERS

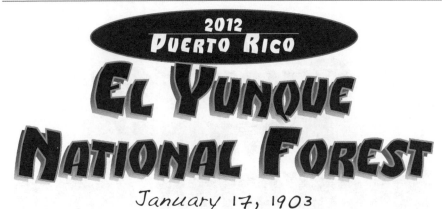

2012
PUERTO RICO
EL YUNQUE
NATIONAL FOREST

January 17, 1903

There are surprises around every bend in the trail at El Yunque National Forest in Puerto Rico," writes Aaron McKeon in *America's Beautiful National Parks.* "With mountain peaks of up to 3,500 feet catching buckets of rainfall every day, El Yunque is like a jade castle rising out of the eastern hills of the island."

This is the only tropical rainforest in the U.S. National Forest system. Its trees, ferns, and other plants enjoy 12 to 16 feet of rain every year–compared to about 1.5 feet in California, 3 feet in New York, or 4 feet in Florida. More than 250 different animal species live in this unique ecosystem. One is the endangered Puerto Rican Amazon parrot; El Yunque is the only place where they live in the wild, and there are only about 40 of them.

High in the Loquillo Mountains, above 2,500 feet, the sun rarely shines through the heavy mist. Because of this, although the trees get constant rain, they rarely grow above 15 feet tall. When you visit El Yunque, look for beautiful orchid flowers and listen for the famous chirp of the tiny coqui frog.

This forest got its name from the area's frequent thunderstorms, which sound like a giant hammer hitting an anvil (yunque in Spanish).

NATIONAL PARK QUARTERS

RIO GRANDE, PUERTO RICO

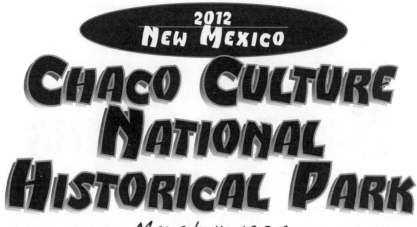

2012
NEW MEXICO
CHACO CULTURE NATIONAL HISTORICAL PARK

March 11, 1907

In northwestern New Mexico is a national park unlike any other. The ancient Hopi and Pueblo cultures who lived here built a complex civilization in and around Chaco Canyon. Their 14 large "Great Houses" had between 100 and 650 rooms each. Large religious chambers called *kivas* were made underground. A sophisticated system delivered water from the natural pools in the surrounding cliffs. Hundreds of miles of roads connected the canyon to other local settlements–roads that are straight, unbending, and precise. Modern Americans didn't realize how straight these roads are until after airplanes were invented and they could be photographed from above.

When you visit Chaco Culture National Historical Park, you leave the modern world behind and learn about people who were like us in some ways, but very different in others.

The United Nations has named this mysterious region a World Heritage site, like the Pyramids of Egypt and the Frontier Regions of the ancient Roman Empire.

The Chaco culture built almost 200 miles of perfectly straight roads. When they came to a canyon or mesa, instead of bending they built a staircase going down or up!

NAGEEZI, NEW MEXICO

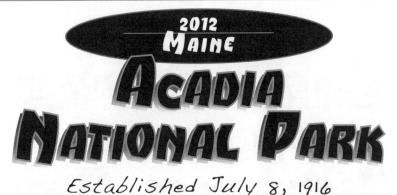

2012 MAINE
ACADIA NATIONAL PARK

Established July 8, 1916

Acadia National Park occupies several islands off Maine, plus a stretch of mainland coast. Here the mountains meet the sea–more than 20 peaks, up to 1,500 feet high. When the French explorer Samuel de Champlain explored the area in 1604, he named the main island Mount Desert, because of its barren, rocky mountaintops.

Acadia has 120 miles of trails in its 48,000 acres. Some are very easy to hike–for others, you need to climb iron rungs and ladders built into the side of Champlain Mountain! More than 50 miles of carriage roads are available for horseback riding, walking, and skiing (but no cars are allowed).

For many years, the coast of Maine was a vacation spot for very wealthy Americans. Today everyone can enjoy its natural beauty in Acadia National Park.

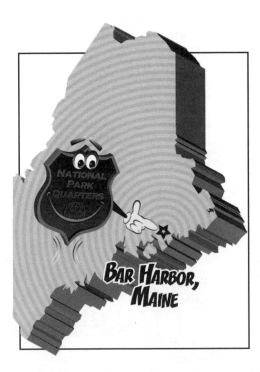

BAR HARBOR, MAINE

The rocks of the mountains here were scraped round and smooth by ancient glaciers.

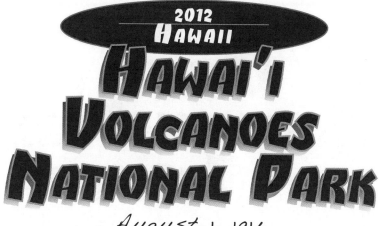

2012 HAWAII
HAWAI'I VOLCANOES NATIONAL PARK

August 1, 1916

Aaron McKeon, in *America's Beautiful National Parks: Collecting the New National Park Quarters,* tells a curious tale: "According to legend, Pele, the volcano goddess, came to Hawaii to find a home. She used a stick to dig pits in the Hawaiian islands, but her water-goddess sister filled each of them with water. When Pele reached Mount Kilauea, on the big island, she dug deeper and her sister was unable to douse the fires. Pele's passions and jealousies produce the mountain's violent eruptions, which continue to this day."

When you explore Hawai'i Volcanoes National Park, you're in Pele's home. Sometimes the roads have to be closed because of hot, flowing lava. Park rangers will warn you about any new cracks in the earth—they can blast out dangerous gases. Lava oozes from the earth and pushes into the Pacific Ocean. The island is constantly growing and shifting.

This fiery, beautiful national park includes Mauna Loa, the largest volcano in the world. Mauna Loa hasn't erupted since 1984—but scientists are keeping a close eye on it!

The fountains of lava for which the park is named actually built these islands in the ocean.

HAWAI'I NATIONAL PARK, HAWAII

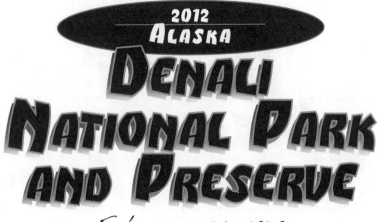

2012
ALASKA
DENALI NATIONAL PARK AND PRESERVE

February 26, 1917

When you hike across the frozen tundra of Denali National Park, you're chilled by frigid winds in a land of glaciers and grizzly bears. The Alaska wilderness is remarkably beautiful–but it is a place to be taken seriously.

Denali is larger than the entire state of Massachusetts. It's famous as the home of Mount McKinley, the highest point on the continent of North America (20,300 feet above sea level). Serious mountain climbers come from all over the world to climb its slopes. For a gentler hike, there are trails on the northeastern end of the park, and more than two million acres of wilderness in this remote and wild region.

Park rangers here use dogsleds to patrol the wilderness in winter.

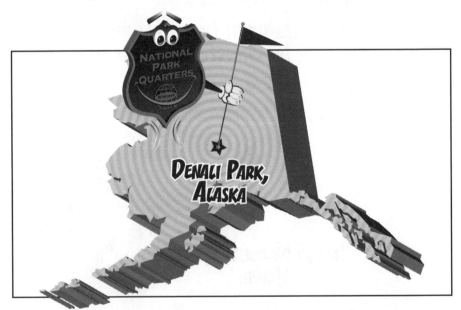

DENALI PARK, ALASKA

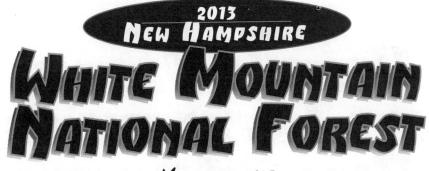

2013
NEW HAMPSHIRE
WHITE MOUNTAIN NATIONAL FOREST

May 16, 1918

Autumn is one of the best times to visit White Mountain National Forest in northern New Hampshire. Birch, sugar maples, American beeches, and other trees explode with brilliant color this time of year.

Mountain climbers hike up the many peaks of the Presidential Range, aiming for the granddaddy of them all, Mount Washington—the highest peak in New England. Inside the park you can also ski, snowboard, and go mountain biking.

The White Mountain region was settled in the 1600s and 1700s. Farmers cleared the land, and loggers cut down trees. Finally, in the early 1900s, conservationist groups convinced the government that the White Mountains deserved to be protected. The National Forest was established by President Woodrow Wilson in 1918, and today it's enjoyed by more than six million visitors every year.

Being close to so many major cities, this is one of the most popular parks to visit.

LACONIA, NEW HAMPSHIRE

PERRY'S VICTORY AND INTERNATIONAL PEACE MEMORIAL

March 3, 1919

In a naval battle during the War of 1812, Captain James Lawrence was shot while commanding the USS *Chesapeake*. As he lay dying, he ordered his men to keep shooting back and not to give up the ship. Lawrence's friend, Commander Oliver Perry, had the inspiring words, "Don't give up the ship," stitched on the blue field of his own battle flag. In September 1813 Perry hoisted the battle flag as he attacked a heavily armed British squadron.

The battle was nearly a disaster for Commander Perry. His flagship was destroyed. Most of his men were killed or wounded. But Perry and four sailors managed to take the flag and row to the nearby USS *Niagara*. Perry commanded the *Niagara* and rallied his squadron, pounding the British ships and forcing them to surrender. "We have met the enemy," he wrote to Brigadier General William Henry Harrison, "and they are ours."

Today, the American victory—and the peacetime that followed the War of 1812—are celebrated at this memorial on South Bass Island in Lake Erie. Under the 352-foot monument, six officers who were killed in the battle are buried. Three are American, and three are British.

PUT-IN-BAY, OHIO

The column on the island is 47 feet higher than the Statue of Liberty—only three other monuments in the United States are taller.

2013
NEVADA
GREAT BASIN NATIONAL PARK

January 24, 1922

Great Basin National Park is in Nevada, due south of U.S. Highway 50–called the Loneliest Road in America. The nearest town is Ely, population about 4,000. The park is far away from any big cities; it only gets about 200 visitors per day (compared to more than 11,000 at the Statue of Liberty).

Great Basin might not attract huge crowds, but it offers its visitors unique experiences. Lehman Caves is a natural wonder, a limestone cavern system full of ancient stalactites and stalagmites. (Here's how to remember the difference: a stalac*tite* holds *tight* to the ceiling of the cave so it doesn't drop.) Wheeler Peak Glacier is one of the southernmost glaciers in the United States.

Another famous feature of the park is its groves of bristlecone pine trees. The Great Basin gets a paltry 6 to 12 inches of rain per year, so only robust shrubs and scrub trees can live there. The bristlecone pine is so used to harsh conditions that it doesn't always add a new ring for every year of growth. It grows slowly and densely. Even though these trees can live 5,000 years or more, they rarely get higher than 30 feet tall–about 1/10 the size of a giant sequoia.

The bristlecone pine tree, a native of Great Basin's rugged mountains, can live 5,000 years or more.

BAKER, NEVADA

FORT MCHENRY NATIONAL MONUMENT AND HISTORIC SHRINE

March 3, 1925

Fort McHenry is where Francis Scott Key, a lawyer from Washington, witnessed the American flag flying after a dramatic 25-hour battle. It was during the War of 1812, and the British had attacked the fort in order to try to get to the city of Baltimore. Their warships could fire cannonballs and rockets far enough to reach the fort, but the fort's guns couldn't reach the ships. Key was being held on a British ship during the attack, which he watched through the night. In the morning, after the British had thrown nearly 2,000 bombs at the fort, Key eagerly scanned the walls to see whose flag was flying: if it was the British flag, then the fort had been overtaken, and the city of Baltimore would be attacked next. Key was delighted to finally see that the U.S. flag–the "star-spangled banner"–was flying over Fort McHenry. The fort's strong walls had survived the British bombardment.

Francis Scott Key was inspired to write "The Defence of Fort McHenry" to celebrate his joy at seeing the American flag still flying. In 1931, a congressional resolution made it the U.S. national anthem.

According to national tradition, when a new U.S. flag is designed, it first flies over Fort McHenry.

2013
SOUTH DAKOTA
MOUNT RUSHMORE NATIONAL MEMORIAL

March 3, 1925

In 1936, President Franklin Roosevelt unveiled the gigantic granite bust of Thomas Jefferson on Mount Rushmore. It was the mountain's second complete portrait, after George Washington's was dedicated in 1934. In 1937 Abraham Lincoln would follow, and then Theodore Roosevelt in 1939. At Jefferson's dedication, the president spoke of the gigantic sculpture's "permanent beauty and permanent importance."

The site of the memorial at Mount Rushmore was established in 1925, and work on the granite mountain began in 1927, deep in the Black Hills of South Dakota—the center of the world, according to the local Lakota Indians. Today, nearly three million visitors come here every year to see the memorial to four of our most important presidents: Washington, the Father of Our Country; Jefferson, who wrote the Declaration of Independence; Lincoln, who saved the Union; and Roosevelt, who ushered in a new era of progress.

Over 90% of the carving on the mountain was made from dynamite, which removed 450,000 tons of rock.

KEYSTONE, SOUTH DAKOTA

2014
TENNESSEE
GREAT SMOKY MOUNTAINS NATIONAL PARK

May 22, 1926

According to one version of the Cherokee story of creation, before there was land, there was only the great stone arch of the sky above endless water. All of the animals lived in the sky, which began to get crowded. The water beetle was brave enough to jump in and swim deep below the surface. He found mud, which he brought up to the surface, and it magically grew to be the earth. Another animal attached the mud to the sky with four rawhide ropes. Then the Great Buzzard flew down to the earth to make it ready. He was tired when he arrived and his wings flapped in the mud, creating mountains and valleys. This became the Cherokee homeland.

The Cherokee were forced out of their lands in 1832 and marched to Oklahoma on the Trail of Tears. The animals remained, however, and today the Smoky Mountains are known as a place of unique biological diversity. Great Smoky Mountains National Park teems with wildlife of all kinds, from bugs to bears. You can also see and study salamanders, rare and endangered plants, and more than 50 native species of trout. Elk, river otters, and peregrine falcons are making a comeback here.

Its rugged scenery, diverse wildlife, 800-plus trails for hiking, and 2,100 miles of streams for fishing attract nine million visitors to Great Smoky Mountains every year, making it the most heavily visited of the national parks.

The "smoke" in these mountains is actually mist, which encourages the growth of diverse plant life.

GATLINBURG, TENNESSEE

NATIONAL PARK QUARTERS

2014
VIRGINIA
SHENANDOAH NATIONAL PARK

May 22, 1926

In 1929 President Herbert Hoover built Rapidan Camp, a "summer White House," in the Blue Ridge Mountains, in what is now Shenandoah National Park. It was a place for the nation's chief executive to get away from the pressures and the spotlight of Washington, D.C.

About 90 miles from the nation's capital, Shenandoah National Park is a refuge of wilderness and mountain peaks tucked into northern Virginia. When you go by car along Skyline Drive, the 105-mile road that runs along the park's spine, you get amazing views of the park and nearby mountains. To explore deeper, you can stay in a rustic park cabin–six of them are available, some built back in the 1920s. Watch for the local wildlife, including bobcats, bears, and the endangered Shenandoah salamander (found only in this park).

This park is in the Blue Ridge Mountains, whose mists give the hills their blue appearance.

LURAY, VIRGINIA

2014
UTAH
ARCHES NATIONAL PARK

April 12, 1929

In *Desert Solitaire,* environmentalist Edward Abbey describes the scenery at Arches National Park as a "monstrous and inhuman spectacle of rock and cloud and sky and space."

More than 200 natural sandstone arches reach into the sky at this park. You can walk trails that lead you deep into the sandstone canyons, getting an up-close look at the Devil's Garden and the base of Delicate Arch. You can even ride your bike and go climbing in the park–but not on any of the arches and features that have names, like Balanced Rock, Courthouse Towers, or Fiery Furnace.

The arches were formed by the slow action of water and ice moving through sandstone, wearing away the younger parts of cliffs, leaving the denser rock to create a bridge or arch. To be considered an arch, the resulting holes must be at least three feet wide, in any direction. Some are as large as 50 feet wide!

No other place in the world has more of the eerie sandstone arches that give this park its name!

MOAB, UTAH

2014
COLORADO
GREAT SAND DUNES NATIONAL PARK

March 17, 1932

For thousands of years, the sand at Great Sand Dunes National Park in south central Colorado has been pitched to the east by prevailing winds and tossed back to the west by storm winds. The winds have built the dunes up, rather than blowing them away–like a potter skillfully turning clay on a wheel to make a graceful bowl.

The sand dunes here in the San Luis Valley are up to 750 feet high, in a field of 85 acres. Rising above the dunes are the snow-capped Sangre de Cristo Mountains.

The Great Sand Dunes aren't a boring desert. You can climb them, roll around in them, and even slide down them in a plastic sled or skis!

This much sand is a valuable natural resource–it could be mixed with cement to make concrete, to construct offices and banks and supermarkets and other buildings. But for more than 70 years, the Great Sand Dunes have been protected from that kind of use, as a national park.

Because of sand falling in the streambed, Medano Creek is constantly shifting its banks.

MOSCA, COLORADO

NATIONAL PARK QUARTERS

2014 FLORIDA — EVERGLADES NATIONAL PARK

May 30, 1934

Water originally covered 11,000 square miles of southern Florida, including what is now the city of Miami. Americans realized the potential value of this region, with its tropical weather and beachfront property. In the late 1800s and early 1900s, the swamps were drained as quickly as possible. Hundreds of miles of canals were built to move the water out of this unique ecosystem.

By the 1920s and early 1930s, people had begun to realize how unusual and special these wetlands were, with their exotic wildlife and plants. Slowly, they convinced others that this was more than just a swamp to be drained to make way for cities and vacation homes. Everglades National Park was the end result—a protected region of 1.5 million acres, a unique wildlife refuge, and the third-largest of the parks in the continental United States.

Threatened and endangered species found here include the Florida panther, the West Indian manatee, four different turtle species, the American alligator, the American crocodile, and the wood stork.

The slow movement of water over the marshes gave the Everglades the nickname "River of Grass."

SOUTHERN FLORIDA

2015
NEBRASKA
HOMESTEAD NATIONAL MONUMENT OF AMERICA

March 19, 1936

The Homestead Act of 1862 affected many Americans' lives. Under this act, hard work and self-reliance would bring success: the government gave 160 acres of Western land (a "homestead") to settlers who promised to develop the property for five years.

When President Abraham Lincoln signed the act, it made 270 million acres available for settlement. This included land west of the Mississippi River (outside of Texas), plus land in Alaska and some "eastern" states like Florida, Mississippi, Alabama, and Ohio. The territory of Nebraska saw the most action: 45 percent of its land was given to hardworking settlers. Homestead National Monument of America, in southeastern Nebraska, was created in 1936 on the site of Daniel Freeman's farm. Freeman filed the very first homestead claim, on January 1, 1863.

This monument reminds us of the grit and determination it took for early Americans to expand our nation and settle the West.

Under the Homestead Act, the government gave away 160-acre parcels of land; the only cost was an $18 filing fee.

BEATRICE, NEBRASKA

2015
LOUISIANA
KISATCHIE NATIONAL FOREST

June 3, 1936

Caroline Dorman, a young teacher from northern Louisiana, in 1919 was sent to teach at the Kisatchie School in the state's backwoods. In the 1920s Ms. Dorman saw how loggers were clearcutting the region's thick forests. She protested, saying that the natural resources should be protected—and her voice was heard. More than 600,000 acres of forest were set aside as a national treasure. Today Kisatchie National Forest has more than 100 miles of hiking trails. You can go mountain biking, hunting, and fishing here, and ride off-road vehicles on some trails. There's also 8,700 acres of wilderness that can be reached only by foot or on horseback—perfect for birdwatching and communing with nature.

The "Louisiana Maneuvers"—war games held in part of Kisatchie National Forest in 1940 and 1941—were important in preparing the U.S. military to fight in World War II.

NATIONAL PARK QUARTERS

PINEVILLE, LOUISIANA

June 30, 1936

For the ultimate national-parks driving experience, take the Blue Ridge Parkway. It stretches from Great Smoky Mountains National Park (in North Carolina) to Skyline Drive in Shenandoah National Forest (in Virginia). This 469-mile roadway is a national park itself.

The Blue Ridge Parkway runs along mountain peaks parallel to the Appalachian Trail. You can see cataracts and historic homes, small mountain villages and national forests. The backdrop for everything is the Appalachian Mountains, rolling away as far as the eye can see. The National Park Service recommends you take your time on the trip–four days–to soak in all its sights and enjoy the experience. You will pass through the Cherokee Indian Reservation, the Nantahala National Forest, Mount Pisgah National Forest, the city of Asheville (with its Folk Art Center), and many other smaller parks, villages, and sites.

The speed limit on the Blue Ridge Parkway is 45 miles per hour. This is not a road for rushing.

Work on this 469-mile highway started in 1935. It took 52 years to complete!

ASHEVILLE, NORTH CAROLINA

2015
DELAWARE
BOMBAY HOOK NATIONAL WILDLIFE REFUGE

June 22, 1937

Do you live on or near North America's Atlantic Coast? If so, the geese you see flying overhead in the spring and fall will probably be making a stop at Bombay Hook National Wildlife Refuge.

This 16,000-acre sanctuary sits on the southern shore of Delaware Bay, where the fresh water of the Delaware River mingles with the Atlantic. It includes about 13,000 acres of tidal salt marsh: a mix of slow-moving water, tidal pools, and mud flats. Human visitors can't see much of this area, but for migratory or nesting birds it provides excellent habitat, rich in vegetation, insects, and crustaceans. How many of its 250 bird species will you spot when you visit? During the fall migration, on their long trip to wintering grounds, about 150,000 ducks and geese stop here to rest.

Believe it or not, many birds love Bombay Hook because of the seafood! In the spring, horseshoe crabs lay their eggs on the beaches and birds dig them up for a feast.

SMYRNA, DELAWARE

Native Americans first sold this land to a Dutch colonist for one gun, four handfuls of powder, three waistcoats, an anchor of alcohol, and a kettle.

2015
NEW YORK
SARATOGA NATIONAL HISTORICAL PARK

June 1, 1938

T he story of the 1777 American victory over the British in the fields and wooded hills near Saratoga, New York, is a classic in military history.

As interesting as it is to read about this Revolutionary War battle, it's even more interesting to actually visit the hills, valleys, and farmhouses in the region where it took place. The battlefield covers about 3,000 acres, and you can drive it on a nine-mile self-guided tour.

This is a place to relive the heroic actions of General John Burgoyne ... Colonel Thaddeus Kosciuszko ... General Horatio Gates ... and thousands of other officers and soldiers, both American and British.

During the Battle of Saratoga, American general Benedict Arnold bravely charged between two British artillery fortifications and was wounded in the leg. More than 100 years later, a monument was built there, showing Arnold's boot! Because Benedict Arnold later became a traitor and betrayed the United States, he was not personally named on the statue. Instead, he is identified as "the most brilliant soldier of the Continental Army"–a description that honors his early service to the nation.

During the Revolutionary War, boys as young as 14 and 15 could hold the rank of lieutenant in the army, putting them in charge of men their dads' age!

STILLWATER, NEW YORK

2016
ILLINOIS
SHAWNEE NATIONAL FOREST

September 6, 1939

In southern Illinois, cornfields and ruler-straight roads are interrupted by the Ozark and Shawnee mountains. Erosion and weathering have created interesting rock formations here, and preservation efforts have allowed forests to reclaim the land. As a result, Shawnee National Forest has become one of the state's most popular places for outdoor recreation.

When you visit, you'll see natural attractions like the Little Grand Canyon, rock outcroppings in the Garden of the Gods and the Devil's Backbone, and waterfalls. Most people like to hike through the forest, but horseback riding is also popular. You can climb, fish, hunt, and camp in the park–but watch out for dangerous wildlife, like copperheads, rattlesnakes, and water moccasins. Other animals that live here include muskrats, fox, and beavers.

This national forest was originally created to help prevent soil erosion along the Ohio and Mississippi rivers.

HARRISBURG, ILLINOIS

2016
KENTUCKY
CUMBERLAND GAP NATIONAL HISTORICAL PARK

June 11, 1940

During the Civil War, Ulysses Grant described the Appalachian Mountains as "the American Gibraltar," like an unbreakable fortress. The Cumberland Gap was a convenient place to cross these rugged mountains–the best crossing for hundreds of miles to the north or south.

To early Americans, the Cumberland Gap was a connection between civilization and the wild western frontier. Decades before the Civil War, frontiersman Daniel Boone had blazed the Wilderness Road through the Gap, and earlier still, the Native Americans had their Warriors' Path, connecting what are now Virginia and North Carolina to Kentucky and Tennessee.

Today, Cumberland Gap National Historical Park sits on 20,000 acres at the intersection of Kentucky, Tennessee, and Virginia. In addition to the Gap itself, you can explore hiking trails through the mountains and take a tour of fascinating caves.

At one time it was proposed that a gigantic head of Abraham Lincoln be carved in the face of the Pinnacle Overlook.

MIDDLESBORO, KENTUCKY

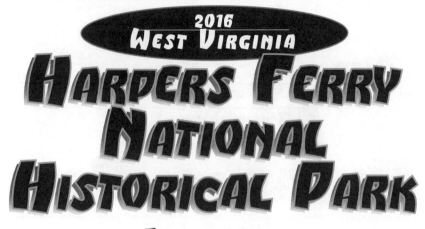

2016
WEST VIRGINIA
HARPERS FERRY
NATIONAL
HISTORICAL PARK

June 30, 1944

If you look down from the surrounding hills to where the Shenandoah and Potomac rivers meet, you'll see a peaceful little community called Harpers Ferry. It's hard to believe this was the scene of violence in the late 1850s.

In October 1859 an abolitionist* named John Brown, leading 21 men, attacked Harpers Ferry. Brown wanted to grab the guns in the town's federal arsenal, and lead an armed revolt of black slaves. Within 36 hours, several men were killed or wounded, and Brown and his fighters were surrounded. He was captured, and later was found guilty of treason and hanged.

Less than two years later, the Civil War broke out. Union soldiers burned the federal arsenal at Harpers Ferry to keep it away from the Confederates. The Confederates destroyed factory buildings and a railroad bridge to keep them from being used by the Union. Eight times during the war the little village went back and forth, first controlled by the North, then by the South, then back again.

In 1906, the first U.S. meeting of the Niagara Movement was held in Harpers Ferry. This group was an early form of the National Association for the Advancement of Colored People (NAACP). One of the reasons Harpers Ferry was chosen for this important meeting was because of its historic connection to John Brown's anti-slavery rebellion.

* abolitionist: someone who wanted to end slavery

John Brown's Fort, the old firehouse in Harpers Ferry, was sent to Chicago in 1891 for the World's Columbian Exposition.

HARPERS FERRY, WEST VIRGINIA

2016
NORTH DAKOTA
THEODORE ROOSEVELT NATIONAL PARK

February 25, 1946

Theodore Roosevelt stepped into the rugged landscape of North Dakota at the age of 25. He was mostly interested in hunting bison. After he met some local ranchers, though, he decided to start a cattle ranch to make money. That plan didn't work out (he built the ranch, but not a profit).

Roosevelt's time as a rancher taught him about the West and Midwest. He saw human settlement moving into the wilderness, affecting its beauty. Years later, when he was president of the United States, Roosevelt created the U.S. Forest Service, approved the 1906 American Antiquities Act (which allowed the creation of national monuments), and protected an estimated 230 million acres of land.

Theodore Roosevelt National Park honors the man and a chapter in his life that shaped how he thought about conservation. It preserves the land and its wildlife. When you visit, you can see prairie dogs, herds of bison, wild mustangs, and golden eagles—much like Teddy Roosevelt did more than a hundred years ago.

A young man who started a ranch in these harsh and beautiful badlands during the 1880s would eventually become president of the United States.

MEDORA, NORTH DAKOTA

2016
SOUTH CAROLINA
FORT MOULTRIE (FORT SUMTER NATIONAL MONUMENT)

April 28, 1948

The wooden logs of the fort on Sullivan's Island were still being put in place when it was attacked by British ships in June 1776. Amazingly the fort was able to withstand the bombardment. If the British had smashing its defenses, they could have sailed into Charleston Harbor and taken South Carolina's capitol city. After the Battle of Sullivan's Island, the fort was named in honor of its commander, Colonel William Moultrie.

After the Revolutionary War, Fort Moultrie declined, was rebuilt, was swept away by a hurricane, and was rebuilt again. On the eve of the Civil War, it was the headquarters for the U.S. Army garrison in Charleston. Because Fort Moultrie was poorly equipped to deal with an attack from land, its strategic importance had largely been eclipsed by the newer Fort Sumter, being built on an island in the middle of the harbor's entrance.

After South Carolina split from the Union, Moultrie and Sumter were the first forts involved in the battle between North and South.

Today, Fort Moultrie is part of Fort Sumter National Monument. When you visit, the Fort Moultrie portion of the park will show you how military technology progressed there over several centuries.

SULLIVAN'S ISLAND, SOUTH CAROLINA

Fort Moultrie defended the U.S. seacoast for 171 years, from 1776 to 1947.

2017
Iowa
Effigy Mounds National Monument

October 25, 1949

On bluffs above the Mississippi River in northeast Iowa are 206 mysterious prehistoric mounds. Nobody is sure why they were built. From the ground, most of them don't look like anything, but from above you can see their shapes.

The oldest mounds at Effigy Mounds National Monument are shaped like cones, and they're about 2,500 years old. They're around 10 to 20 feet in diameter, but not unusually tall–between 2 feet and 8 feet high. The strangest ones are the large "effigy" mounds (an effigy is a figure or image). Most of them are shaped like bears or birds. One of the bird mounds has a wingspan of 212 feet! The Great Bear Mound is less than 4 feet high, but is 137 feet long and 70 feet wide.

According to Native American tradition, the mounds were sacred ceremonial sites. They might have been used for burials.

When you visit Effigy Mounds National Monument, remember that you're in a special place, a sacred burial site. You won't find fancy observation towers or noisy tour groups–just quiet trails under basswood and sugar maples, and the mystery of the ancient mounds.

Of the 200-plus mounds here, 31 are in the shapes of animals.

HARPERS FERRY, IOWA

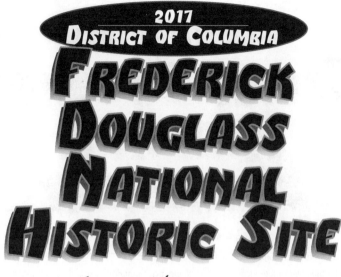

2017
DISTRICT OF COLUMBIA
FREDERICK DOUGLASS NATIONAL HISTORIC SITE

September 5, 1962

Frederick Douglass was a slave who made two unsuccessful attempts to escape. On his third try, in 1838, he finally made his way to freedom. He had borrowed some papers that identified him as a free black man in the U.S. Navy; disguised as a sailor, he hopped on a train in Maryland and made his way to Philadelphia and then to New York City, where there was no slavery. He married a free black woman, Anna Murray, who he'd met earlier in Maryland.

Douglass went on to become one of the most influential Americans of the 19th century. He traveled the country (and overseas) speaking against slavery, telling people how the "peculiar institution" hurt both slaves and their masters. He published an anti-slavery newspaper, *The North Star*, and wrote books. In addition to fighting against slavery, he also spoke in favor of women's rights, convincing many people that every American should be free and equal.

Today you can explore Douglass's house in Anacostia in Washington, D.C. This was his home after the Civil War, from 1878 until he died in 1895.

Frederick Douglass was a close friend of Abraham Lincoln's. He convinced Lincoln to free the slaves, resulting in the Emancipation Proclamation.

WASHINGTON, D.C.

2017
MISSOURI
OZARK NATIONAL SCENIC RIVERWAYS

August 27, 1964

Ozark National Scenic Riverways was the first national park founded to protect a wild river system. Its rivers are fed by more than 300 springs, including the largest concentration of first-magnitude springs in the world. A first-magnitude spring has a flow of at least 65 million gallons of water per day. (The Big Spring has a daily water flow of 286 million gallons!) The springs are a beautiful shade of blue.

When you visit, you can see some of the park's hundreds of caves. The magnificent Jam Up Cave can be reached only by boat. Rangers lead tours of Round Spring Cavern every day during the summer.

Many kinds of animals are attracted to the springs and caves. There are rare species of fish, found only in the Ozarks. You might see white-tailed deer and wild turkeys. Look out for collared lizards, tarantulas, and scorpions!

Other sites to explore include the ruins of an old hospital, a mill built in 1894, a one-room schoolhouse, and an old-fashioned general store. You can go camping (in tents or cabins), and hunting and fishing are allowed in some parts of the park. The most fun might be the famous floating trip down the spring-fed rivers, and you can also rent a canoe to paddle around.

The bluffs near the Jacks Forks River are home to many rare plants left there from the last ice age; these plants are extinct in other parts of the state.

VAN BUREN, MISSOURI

NATIONAL PARK QUARTERS

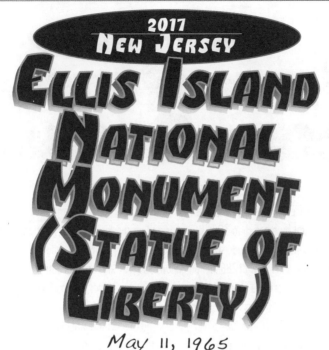

2017
NEW JERSEY
ELLIS ISLAND NATIONAL MONUMENT (STATUE OF LIBERTY)

May 11, 1965

Years ago, a girl named Annie Moore was welcomed into Ellis Island Immigration Station. It was a cold New Year's Day, 1892, and it happened to be Annie's 15th birthday. She had come from County Cork, Ireland, with her two little brothers, to join their parents in Manhattan. Annie Moore was the very first immigrant to enter the United States through Ellis Island. By the time it closed in 1952, 12 million others had followed her.

People came to the United States from Europe to get away from wars, violence, and not enough food. They saw America as the land of opportunity. Ellis Island was set up as a place to control the flow of poor Europeans and other people coming into the country. (Wealthier travelers would have their immigration papers approved on board their ship, and didn't have to go through the lines at Ellis Island.) If you were sick, or unable to support yourself, or a criminal, you would be turned away. If you were healthy, and had your papers in order, you could pass through Ellis Island in three or four hours. After that, the promise of America awaited you.

NATIONAL PARK QUARTERS

ELLIS ISLAND, NEW JERSEY

The Statue of Liberty is made of copper only as thick as two pennies put together.

2017
INDIANA
GEORGE ROGERS CLARK NATIONAL HISTORICAL PARK

July 23, 1966

In February 1779 George Rogers Clark, a young lieutenant colonel in the Virginia militia, led 130 men on a 180-mile march through the wilderness to Fort Sackville, in Indiana. British soldiers who controlled the fort, along with their Indian allies, had been raiding American settlements. Clark wanted to stop them.

Because it was winter, the British commander, Henry Hamilton, had let some of his guards go home until spring. He was very surprised to discover that his fort was surrounded by Clark and his men. Knowing the fort was poorly defended, and after seeing some of their Indian allies killed, the British surrendered.

George Rogers Clark National Historical Park is a monument to the fighting spirit of America's early patriots. Control of Fort Sackville helped guarantee the United States' control of the frontier throughout the Revolutionary War. In 1814, years after the war ended, the British finally gave up their claim to the Northwest Territory.

This park memorializes a Revolutionary War battle for Fort Sackville, but nobody knows the actual location of the fort today.

VINCENNES, INDIANA

2018
MICHIGAN
PICTURED ROCKS
NATIONAL
LAKESHORE

October 15, 1966

Forty-two miles of Lake Superior shoreline are preserved in Pictured Rocks National Lakeshore. The star attractions at this park are the colorful 200-foot sandstone cliffs rising above the water. Waterfalls tumble into the lake. The scenery is some of the best that Lake Superior can offer.

Pictured Rocks was the first designated national lakeshore. The park also preserves nearly 34,000 acres of Michigan's Upper Peninsula. You can walk the short trails that lead to sites such as Grand Sable Dunes, covering five square miles on the park's northeastern end, and Miner's Castle, the park's most famous rock formation. You can also take a boat tour on Beaver Lake, Little Beaver Lake, or Grand Sable Lake.

Fill up your backpack and hike around the lakeshore's forests, waterfalls, and wetlands. You should see plenty of wild animals; be on the lookout for moose, lynx, red fox, and badgers.

The shipwrecks of Lake Superior's "Graveyard Coast" represent many eras of shipping. Most are very well preserved.

2018
WISCONSIN
APOSTLE ISLANDS NATIONAL LAKESHORE

September 26, 1970

The best way to get to know Apostle Islands National Lakeshore is by boat. True, there are more than 50 miles of trails in the park–but most of them are on the islands! Only one trail is on the mainland. In the summer, experienced paddlers take their sea kayaks out to explore the park's many islands and the mainland's sea caves. Stockton Island is home to one of the largest concentrations of black bears in North America. When you visit, you're likely to see more than 20 of them.

In the freezing winter the sea caves turn into *ice* caves, and you can explore them by foot. Check with the Visitor's Center; they'll tell you how thick the ice is, and whether it's safe to walk on.

Scuba diving is another popular activity in this park. It's another way to get into the islands' sea caves and the only way to see underwater rock formations, like submerged sandstone ledges. It is also the only way to explore the shipwrecks sitting on the bottom of the lake near the islands.

This lakeshore has more lighthouses than any other National Park Service area– eight towers on six islands.

2018
MINNESOTA
VOYAGEURS
NATIONAL PARK

January 8, 1971

Jacques de Noyon was a French-Canadian fur trader who explored the Rainy Lakes region, west of Lake Superior, more than 300 years ago. We can imagine he saw moose browsing on shrubs in the marshy lowlands. He heard packs of timber wolves howling at the moon. He followed the tracks of beaver, fox, muskrat, and other fur-bearing animals.

Today all of these wilderness experiences remain for you. You can rent a canoe or a rowboat, and explore the region just like a *voyageur*.

The area known today as Voyageurs National Park, on the Minnesota-Canada border, was preserved, largely, thanks to the efforts of Ernest Oberholtzer, one of the founding members of the Wilderness Society. Oberholtzer came to Rainy Lake in the early 1900s. He loved to canoe on the lakes, and he decided to live there in 1915. He later convinced Congress that the area should be protected.

The voyageurs were French-Canadian fur traders who canoed through the lakes and waterways in this region.

2018
GEORGIA
CUMBERLAND ISLAND NATIONAL SEASHORE

October 23, 1972

At Cumberland Island there are no mountains to hike up, no caves to climb down into, no deserts to march across. Your recreation here is walking on white-sand beaches, swimming, looking for sharks' teeth in the surf, and relaxing. Bring a bucket, because you can take as many as two gallons of seashells home with you.

"After you reach Cumberland Island," writes Aaron McKeon in *America's Beautiful National Parks*, "it's you, the waves, the wildlife, and a 17-mile-long island waiting to be explored."

There are 50 miles of hiking trails (a lot for such a small island), including the north-south Grand Avenue, which takes you through a living tunnel of healthy oak boughs. At the northern end of the island is the area known as The Settlement, where black workers lived beginning in the 1890s. One of the remaining structures is the tiny First African Baptist Church.

Do you like to explore mysterious old buildings? The ruins of Dungeness, a mansion built by the Carnegie family, are on the island's southern end, just above the marshes and ponds at the tip of the island. It was built on the site of an earlier mansion of the same name, which fell apart in the years after the Civil War.

Cumberland Island is almost completely undeveloped; only 300 people are allowed on the island at a time, and motor vehicles are forbidden.

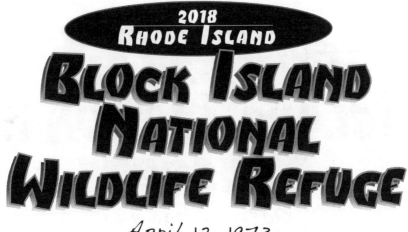

2018
RHODE ISLAND
BLOCK ISLAND NATIONAL WILDLIFE REFUGE

April 12, 1973

If you like birds and butterflies, this park is for you. Block Island National Wildlife Refuge is a resting place for migratory songbirds using the Atlantic flyway. Small birds that get pushed off their southern route by strong winds can land here. The island gives them a chance to eat and rest before continuing on their journey.

In spring and fall, you can hear the trill of the song sparrow and the calls of 70 other songbird species. In summer, you'll see tiger swallowtail and other butterflies; and late September brings the annual monarch butterfly migration.

There are no marked trails in the refuge. You can explore to your heart's content.

NEW SHOREHAM, RHODE ISLAND

Block Island was named by The Nature Conservancy as one of "The Last Great Places" in the Western Hemisphere.

2019
MASSACHUSETTS
LOWELL NATIONAL HISTORICAL PARK

June 5, 1978

In the early 1800s, Massachusetts was a center of the Industrial Revolution in America. Its mills, powered by water drawn in by a system of canals, were cutting-edge technology for their time. Its machines—looms that harnessed the water power and made cotton into textiles—were very productive. Business was so good that companies built large dormitories for their workers (mostly young women, called "Mill Girls") to live in. The town of Lowell was named after a successful businessman; it was a factory town built for the Boston Manufacturing Company.

Between 1820 and 1850, dozens of mills sprouted up in Lowell, drawing thousands of new workers to the area and forever changing how things were made in America. Lowell National Historical Park was established in the 1970s. It preserves an important part of American history.

In the 1850s the mills here produced enough cloth each year to circle the earth twice!

2019
NORTHERN MARIANA ISLANDS
AMERICAN MEMORIAL PARK

August 18, 1978

At Saipan, during World War II, about 70,000 Americans fought 30,000 Japanese soldiers using weapons ranging from fast modern battleships to flamethrowers and bayonets. When the battle was over after three weeks, 13,000 Americans had been killed and wounded and nearly all the Japanese were dead.

American Memorial Park honors the American servicemen and Marianas natives who died in this important battle. These memorials include a court of honor listing the names of more than 5,000 service personnel who died during the Marianas Campaign, and a carillon bell tower that chimes every half hour.

In this park, you can take part in activities that young men and women of the 1940s would have enjoyed, like a baseball game on the park's specially built field, a tennis match on one of the four lighted courts, sunbathing on the white-sand beaches, or a concert at the park's large amphitheater. You can jog or ride a bicycle on the well-tended paths, or go windsurfing at Micro Beach, considered one of the world's best.

The names of more than 5,000 American servicemen who died in Operation Forager are inscribed on a memorial here.

SAIPAN, NORTHERN MARIANA ISLANDS

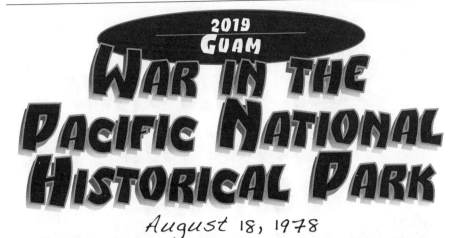

2019
GUAM
WAR IN THE PACIFIC NATIONAL HISTORICAL PARK

August 18, 1978

Guam, a 200-square-mile island in the western Pacific, was the site of some of the fiercest fighting in World War II. Three days after the December 7, 1941, attack on Pearl Harbor, Japanese special forces landed on Guam and overwhelmed the lightly armed U.S. Marines, Guardsmen, and Navy personnel holding the island. Three years later, the Americans returned in force. On July 21, 1944, the first Marines landed. By the time the battle ended on August 4, more than 7,000 Americans had been killed or wounded. More than 18,000 Japanese soldiers died fighting.

The American victory at Guam was one of the turning points in the war in the Pacific. This national park honors the bravery and sacrifices of all who participated in Pacific battles, including the Japanese.

The park includes more than 100 historical sites from the World War II, including bunkers, pill boxes, and defensive guns. In addition, it is a place of great natural beauty. Scuba diving and snorkeling are permitted in the warm Pacific waters. When you visit, you might see the endangered hawksbill sea turtle, the threatened green sea turtle, or 3,500 other marine species.

At the time of the American invasion in 1944, the Japanese were using Asan Beach as a rice-paddy field.

HAGÅTÑA, GUAM

2019 TEXAS
SAN ANTONIO MISSIONS NATIONAL HISTORICAL PARK

November 10, 1978

In the early 1690s, six missions were built along the San Antonio River as outposts of the Catholic Church and of the kingdom of Spain. The Spanish wanted to make sure that Britain and France knew who owned the land, and didn't try to trespass. Most of the missions were fairly large compounds, with high walls and gates to protect against raids by hostile Indian tribes, such as the Apache.

The Franciscan friars who lived in the missions wanted to spread Christianity and Spanish culture to the Native Americans. The small local tribes *(Coahuiltecans)* in eastern Texas and northern Mexico were being pushed south by the Apache, and north by Spanish colonists. The missions were a safe refuge in the middle.

Today four of the original missions are preserved in San Antonio Missions National Historical Park. Each one is still a parish of the Catholic Church. You can visit them by walking a trail along the river in the heart of historic San Antonio. Another famous mission nearby is San Antonio de Valero–better known as the Alamo.

SAN ANTONIO, TEXAS

The first Western cattle drives originated from these missions to help supply colonists during the American Revolution.

2019
IDAHO

FRANK CHURCH RIVER OF NO RETURN WILDERNESS

July 23, 1980

The Wilderness Act of 1964 defines a wilderness, in part, as a place "where man himself is a visitor who does not remain." Since the act was signed by President Lyndon Johnson, about nine million acres of American land have been set aside as wilderness.

Frank Church was a Democratic senator from Idaho, who sponsored the Wilderness Act and also the Wild and Scenic Rivers Act. In 1980 he helped create the River of No Return Wilderness. It was renamed in his honor a few years later. Spreading over 2.3 million acres, it's the largest wilderness area in the continental United States, made up of mountains, canyonlands, rivers, and six national forests in central Idaho. If you love to explore the outdoors, there are 2,600 miles of Forest Service trails, and if you like camping, hunting, and fishing, they're all permitted. If you just want to get away and commune with Nature, this is your place: as the U.S. Forest Service describes it, "opportunities for solitude abound."

The "River of No Return" is the fast-moving Salmon River, a popular location for whitewater rafting.

SALMON, IDAHO

2020
AMERICAN SAMOA
NATIONAL PARK OF AMERICAN SAMOA

October 31, 1988

The National Park of American Samoa is on the other side of the world–an exciting tropical world of coral reefs and volcanic mountains in the South Pacific. American Samoa itself is a chain of seven islands formed when volcanoes pushed up from the ocean floor, up through the water, and up even higher into the sky.

The 13,500-acre park is spread over three different islands. It includes cloud forests (similar to the ones seen in El Yunque in Puerto Rico), beautiful, clean beaches, and reefs full of fish and other tropical water life. One hiking trail goes up Mount Alava, all the way to the top at 1,600 feet. The climb back down, going to the village of Vatia at the mountain's northern base, is so steep you need ladders to get down. To get to the cloud forest on Ta'u island, and to the 350 acres of park on Ofu island, you go island-hopping in a plane.

This is one of the most remote areas in the National Park System. In 2005, the National Park of American Samoa only had about 400 visitors! Camping is not allowed, but if you contact the National Park Service in advance, you can stay with a Samoan family–a great way to get to know the local culture.

This park is actually located on three separate islands–and about 25% of the park is under water!

PAGO PAGO, AMERICAN SAMOA

2020 CONNECTICUT

WEIR FARM NATIONAL HISTORIC SITE

October 31, 1990

Painter J. Alden Weir wrote to a friend in November 1902, telling how important the land was to his art. His "hope and desire" was "to get close to Nature, to know her character more intimately." Weir and nine other painters had started holding their own exhibitions in the late 1890s, to protest other artists' focus on "too much business and not enough art."

This farm in Connecticut was Weir's summer home and studio for 37 years. Its rolling hills and charming stone walls inspired his creativity; he made more than 250 paintings here. Today the farm is a national historic site where you can look into Weir's studio, learn about his artwork, and create your own paintings and drawings of the beautiful surroundings.

This is the only National Park Service site dedicated to American painting.

WILTON, CONNECTICUT

2020
U.S. VIRGIN ISLANDS
SALT RIVER BAY NATIONAL HISTORICAL PARK AND ECOLOGICAL PRESERVE

February 24, 1992

In 1493 Christopher Columbus explored the eastern shore of Salt River Bay, looking for fresh drinking water, on his second voyage to the New World. The local Carib Indians shot at his men with arrows, and they were forced to retreat. Over the years, the Dutch, English, Spanish, French, and Danes all tried to build colonies here. Tropical diseases and wars made it difficult for any single nation to keep control for very long.

Denmark owned the Virgin Islands from 1754 to 1917, and made a lot of money from sugarcane there, harvested by slaves. When slavery was abolished in the Danish colonies, and when more people started making sugar out of beets rather than sugarcane, the islands weren't as profitable for Denmark. The United States bought the islands for $25 million in 1917.

The National Park Service describes the Salt River Bay (on the island of St. Croix) as "a living museum"– a dynamic, tropical ecosystem with prehistoric and colonial-era archeological sites and ruins. When you visit, you'll see some of the largest mangrove forests in the Virgin Islands, as well as coral reefs and an underwater canyon.

CHRISTIANSTED,
VIRGIN-ISLANDS

The coral reefs here protect the shoreline against erosion from large waves caused by hurricanes and heavy storms.

2020
VERMONT
MARSH-BILLINGS-ROCKEFELLER NATIONAL HISTORICAL PARK

August 26, 1992

Many people consider George Perkins Marsh (1801-1882) to be America's first environmentalist. His book, *Man and Nature*, launched the modern conservation movement. Today his childhood home in Vermont is part of Marsh-Billings-Rockefeller National Historical Park.

The Marsh mansion was built in 1805, and the family owned it until Frederick Billings bought it in 1869. Billings had read *Man and Nature*, and George Perkins Marsh was one of his heroes. Billings was a business-man and also a conservationist; one of his ideas was to buy bankrupt farms in Vermont and replant them with trees. He started a dairy and planted a forest around Marsh's old home–it might be the oldest man-aged forest in the United States. Nearly 15 miles of carriage roads built in the 1880s weave around the gentle slopes and historic woodlands of this historic old property.

The Pogue, a man-made pond located in the park, is rumored to be bottomless!

WOODSTOCK, VERMONT

NATIONAL PARK QUARTERS

2020
KANSAS
TALLGRASS PRAIRIE NATIONAL PRESERVE

November 12, 1996

Before Americans moved west and started to build farms between the Mississippi River and the Rocky Mountains, the area was a huge blanket of wild grass–140 million acres of prairie. Today, 96% of the prairieland has been plowed under and developed. When you visit Tallgrass Prairie National Preserve and wade out into the "sea of grass," you get a feel for what it must have looked like back in the early 1800s.

The limestone hills of eastern Kansas weren't good for growing crops, so in 1878 rancher Stephen Jones bought 7,000 acres for his cattle to graze on. He used limestone from the hills to build a mansion and a three-story barn. Over the years, the ranch changed hands and grew to 11,000 acres. This slice of America's old prairie features a nature trail, a historic one-room schoolhouse, and the old Jones mansion and farm buildings. In the future, the park plans to re-introduce herds of bison, like the ones that used to graze the prairie by the tens of millions.

In prehistoric times, this prairie lay at the bottom of a vast, but shallow, inland sea.

NATIONAL PARK QUARTERS

COTTONWOOD FALLS, KANSAS

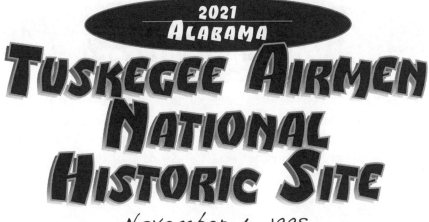

2021
ALABAMA
TUSKEGEE AIRMEN NATIONAL HISTORIC SITE

November 6, 1998

Not every site in the National Park quarters program is a wilderness area, mountain, or seashore. Some are smaller, manmade places of great historical importance.

A perfect example is Tuskegee Airmen National Historic Site, located at Moton Field, a small airport in rural Alabama. This is where the Army Air Force trained the first African American fighter pilots, during World War II. Before that, the military was slow to promote black soldiers to officer level.

The first all-black air unit, the 99th Fighter Squadron, saw combat in June 1943. Soon other black squadrons were flying out of Tuskegee, and they formed the 332nd Fighter Group. The 332nd flew 15,500 sorties and completed nearly 1,600 raids against the enemy. The group was highly respected, earning the Distinguished Unit Citation for heroism. Perhaps more importantly, the graduates of the Tuskegee Army Air Field program proved that black Americans can serve with distinction, just like any other Americans. Benjamin O. Davis Jr., the commander of the 99th Fighter Squadron, went on to become the first black general in the U.S. Air Force.

During World War II, America's first black military pilots were trained here.

TUSKEGEE, ALABAMA

NATIONAL PARK QUARTERS

POCKET CHANGE YOU CAN COLLECT

ach year the U.S. Mint makes the Lincoln cent, the Jefferson nickel, the Roosevelt dime, the Washington quarter, the Kennedy half dollar, the Sacagawea / Native American dollar, and the Presidential
dollar. These modern dollars are sometimes called "golden dollars," but they don't really contain any
gold–they're made mostly of copper and zinc, with a little nickel and manganese. The metals combine to
make a golden color.

Lincoln Cents (1909 to Date)

The Lincoln obverse (top row, center) has been the same since 1909—only the reverses have
changed. The "wheat" reverse (top row, left) was used from 1909 through 1958, while the
Memorial reverse (top row, right) was used from 1959 through 2008. Four new
reverses celebrated the bicentennial of Lincoln's birth in 2009; the designs
(middle row), from left to right, represented his birth and early childhood in
Kentucky, his formative years in Indiana, his professional life in Illinois, and
his presidency in Washington, D.C. Starting in 2010, the reverse represents
Lincoln's unification of the country after the Civil War (right).

Jefferson Nickels (1938 to date)

The original obverse and reverse (left column) were unchanged for more than 65 years.
Then, in 2004, the Westward Journey Nickels Series™ (top row, middle three images)
began; it continued through 2005 (bottom row, middle three images) and into 2006. Since
the end of that series, another new portrait of Thomas Jefferson has looked out at the viewer,
and an updated view of Monticello has appeared on the reverse (right column).

Roosevelt Dimes (1946 to Date)

Today's dime was designed shortly after President Roosevelt died. At first, the mintmark was placed on the reverse, at the bottom of the torch—but in 1968, the Mint changed the location to the obverse, above the date.

Washington Quarters (1932 to Date)

When this coin was first made in 1932, George Washington would have been 200 years old. That original design (left pair) was used all the way up through 1975; then, in 1976, the reverse design changed to celebrate our nation's Bicentennial. The design for that year (right pair) shows a colonial drummer and a victory torch surrounded by 13 stars, one for each of the original colonies that started the United States. In 1977 the old design returned, and the quarter stayed the same until 1998.

In recent years there have been so many special designs on the reverse of the Washington quarter, we couldn't fit them all in this book! Starting in 1999, the Mint began a new program to honor each of the 50 states, and eventually the District of Columbia and the five U.S. territories. A new program began in 2010 to commemorate the national parks and historic sites throughout the country. A sampling of these designs is shown above. By the end of the Mint's program honoring our beautiful national parks, there will be at least 114 Washington quarter designs you can collect.

Kennedy Half Dollar (1964 to Date)

This coin was designed to honor President John F. Kennedy, who was killed in 1963. The design (left) has been the same each year except 1976, when it changed to celebrate the United States Bicentennial (right). The obverse for that year only has the dates "1776–1976," and the reverse design shows Independence Hall in Philadelphia.

Modern Dollars (2000 to Date)

The Native American dollar (top row, left and center) pictures Sacagawea on the obverse and, through 2008, an eagle on the reverse each year. Starting in 2009, the obverse is the same, but each year a different reverse honors an aspect of Native American life (top row, right). These dollars continue to be made at the same time as the Presidential dollars, which began in 2007. Each year until 2016, four different presidents, like George Washington, Thomas Jefferson, John Quincy Adams, and Andrew Jackson (middle row), will be honored on these "golden" dollars. The Statue of Liberty (bottom row, left) appears on the reverse. The edges of Presidential dollars are lettered: in 2007 and 2008 the date, mintmark, and legends were all stamped into the edges (bottom row, right). In 2009 the legend IN GOD WE TRUST was moved to the obverse.

OLDER COINS YOU CAN COLLECT

Here are some older U.S. coins you can collect. You would have to be very lucky to find these coins in your pocket change! But you can easily buy them from a coin dealer or hobby shop.

**Indian Head Cent
(1859–1909)**
Before the Abraham Lincoln design, the one-cent coin featured Miss Liberty in a Native American headdress.

**Indian Head Nickel
(1913–1938)**
Also known as the "Buffalo" nickel, this five-cent coin shows an American bison on the reverse.

**Winged Liberty Dime
(1916–1945)**
People thought that Miss Liberty, with her winged cap, looked like the Roman god Mercury, so this coin is often called the "Mercury" dime.

**Standing Liberty Quarter
(1916–1930)**
Miss Liberty carries a shield, showing that she can protect herself from enemies. But she also holds an olive branch, a symbol of peace.

Franklin Half Dollar (1948–1963)
Founding Father Benjamin Franklin occupied the half dollar before John F. Kennedy. On the reverse we see the Liberty Bell.

Join a Club

You've started collecting and learning about coins. Now you should think about joining a coin club, association, or society! There are many such groups throughout the United States and Canada. Some of them are local clubs that meet one or twice a month, hold coin shows and auctions, and put on presentations for and by members. Others are larger national groups that communicate mainly through newsletters, email, and once-a-year meetings. And some are national or international clubs with thousands of members and smaller, state-based chapters. Many of these groups welcome young collectors and even have special "Young Numismatist" meetings and activities. Older members know that new collectors are the future of the hobby, and they enjoy sharing their knowledge and experience.

Here are some national groups you might be interested in.

American Numismatic Association. *www.money.org.* One of the largest numismatic organizations in the world, the ANA has more than 30,000 members. It promotes studying and collecting money for research, interpretation, and preservation of history and culture from ancient times to the present.

Canadian Numismatic Association. *www.canadian-numismatic.org.* Many U.S. coin collectors also collect coins of our neighbor to the north. The CNA promotes fellowship, communication, and education, and provides advocacy and leadership for the hobby.

Civil War Token Society. *www.cwtsociety.com.* The CWTS encourages interest and research in the field of Civil War tokens, through the Civil War Token Journal, auctions, a reference library, regional meetings, etc.

Colonial Coin Collectors Club. *www.colonialcoins.org.* This club provides a forum for collectors of numismatic material related to the Early American era–coins, tokens, currency, and medals.

CONECA. *www.conecaonline.org.* CONECA is devoted to error- and variety-coin collectors. It focuses on specialties such as doubled dies, repunched mintmarks, double strikes, and off-centered coins.

Early America Coppers. *www.eacs.org.* EAC connects collectors of early U.S. copper coins–colonials, half cents, large cents, and Hard Time tokens. *Penny-Wise* is its bi-monthly magazine.

Numismatic Bibliomania Society. *www.coinbooks.org.* The NBS supports and promotes the use and collecting of numismatic literature–books, periodicals, catalogs, and other written or printed material. Its journal is *The Asylum.*

Society of Paper Money Collectors. *www.spmc.org.* The SPMC is open to anyone interested in paper money or related areas such as checks, stocks, tickets, and engravings. *Paper Money Magazine* is its journal.

Token and Medal Society. *www.tokenandmedal.org.* This educational society promotes the study and collecting of exonumia–tokens, medals, badges, and other related items. Its magazine is the *TAMS Journal.*